A GUERILLA ARTIST'S
PATH TO INDEPENDENCE

CREATURE
W/DAX-DEVLON ROSS

Outskirts Press, Inc.
Denver, Colorado

The Underdog's Manifesto
A Guerilla Artist's Path to Independence
All Rights Reserved
Copyright © 2007 Creature and Dax-Devlon Ross
VR1.0

Outskirts Press
http://www.outskirtspress.com

ISBN-10: 1-4327-0293-9
ISBN-13: 978-1-4327-0293-9

Outskirts Press and the "OP" logo are trademarks belonging to Outskirts Press, Inc.

Printed in the United States of America

I look up to Creature...and he's younger than me! I admire his wit, positive attitude and hard work ethic. He reminds me of ex-Jets running back Matt Snell."

- Ricky Powell
Legendary Hip-Hop photographer and
author of *Oh Snap!* and *The Rickford Files*

With the record industry collapsing and choking on its own vomit of karma, hustling your own work is the way of the future. Can you imagine Jay-Z selling his own work on his own website? Creature can.

- 2 Mex
Underground Hip-Hop Impressario

"Over the years I've peddled thousands of CDs hand to hand, but I've never remotely matched the hustle that is exuded and embodied in Creature."

- Busdriver
Avante-Garde Hip-Hop Artist

"Don't forget to have fun...it's just music!"

- J-Zone, Rapper, Producer
CEO of Old Maid Entertainment

DEDICATION

To any and everybody who's ever felt like an underdog

CONTENTS

FOREWORD

The Underdog's Manifesto was written over the course of roughly four months. Each Thursday at the same time Creature and I met for two hours to write one chapter and to edit the previous week's chapter. We had a plan and a deadline and we stuck to it because we all know what happens when we don't grab hold of our ideas: someone else comes along and takes them. It's no secret anymore that hip-hop has been co-opted by corporate interests. What we wanted to ensure by writing this book was that someone didn't do the same to the independent grind (water it down; glamour it up) before the people who are actually living it had their say. That, at the end of the day, was our driving force. On the days I didn't want to work, Creature pushed me and vice versa. Both of us knew all too well how easy it would be to put this project on hold. We were not being paid by a publishing house to write this book nor did we know if there would be an audience that wanted to read it once we were done. All we knew was that it felt right and that it had to be done.

Over the months of writing *Underdog,* what began for me as a fascination with the independent art scene evolved into an appreciation for the hard work and dedication it takes to come out on the street everyday and put yourself and your work out there to be scrutinized by strangers. I became a believer not just in the hustle itself but in the deeper implications of supporting independent art in an age when it's too easy not to. We live in an increasingly isolated and fractured society that is mediated by technology filtered down by corporate behemoths whose interests are invariably hostile to anything independent. Whether we're aware of it or not we're taught to believe that the word "independent" means "knock-off." Even though we've been hoodwinked time and time again we continue to buy into the culture of corporate hype whereby a high-profile marketing scheme automatically equals a high-quality product. Conversely, if a guy is standing on the corner selling his own product then he must be "whack," otherwise he'd be on television, in magazines, inside Tower and Virgin rather than standing out front. The truth of the matter is that the market is only designed to catapult a handful of people into stardom, and that generally those people have to fit a certain mold or have a certain popular appeal. Again, I don't think I'm saying anything new. Ultimately, talent is only part of the equation that constitutes commercial success.

So what am I trying to say here? Exactly what's my point? My point is that some of the most authentic, audacious and original art being produced today is without question independent and that we have to choose to support it rather than dismiss it just because the creators are standing on street corners. The inimitable Too $hort got his start selling tapes out of paper bags in Oakland. As Duo Live's Fre pointed out in my interview with the group, before Bob Marley became a legend he once hustled his music on the streets of Trenchtown. There's a long and storied history of independent artists being marginalized because the mainstream marketplace didn't believe they were viable. Today's independent artists are merely the latest manifestation of a continuing cycle. My other point is that there's a heckuva lot we can all learn from artists like Creature. In an age where technology allows us to easily avoid contact with one another, the independent artist fights against the tide of complacency and self-doubt every day. To do what they do takes a tremendous amount of courage and humility. It requires them to put their egos aside and to relate to people from all walks of life, something most of us aren't comfortable doing even though we tend to believe otherwise. Having spent many afternoons and evenings working the streets with Creature and his loose knit network of fellow artists these past few months has inspired me as an author. Seeing them interact with strangers has made me want to step out from behind my computer and seek out my audience as well.

You're probably thinking all the lofty talk of ideas and principles is great but is there any real money to be made on the streets. There is. There are thousands of open-minded people who are willing to give you a chance, the key is understanding that this is a business like any other. There are rules one has to follow not only to be individually successful but to preserve and hopefully enhance the integrity of independent art in general. *The Underdog's Manifesto* is both a guidebook and a motivational tool for doing just that. All the voices that speak in this book are sharing their wisdom because they believe the game should be passed along, kept alive. Just as the Chitlin' Circuit was once the breeding ground for generations of popular black artists, the streets are the perfect place for today's "indie" artists to get their start.

I want to say a few words about my co-author before I cede the floor. From the time I first approached him about writing this book, Creature stressed that he was only a representative of the street hustle, a spokesman, not by any means the alpha and omega. He insisted on involving street legends like Percee P. and groups like Duo Live and The Third Message because their knowledge and experience has shaped him. At the end of the day this book is about the hustle, the grind, not any single individual. It's about paying respect to the street itself and to those who've dedicated years of their lives to their art. It is my hope that by reading this book you will gain a greater appreciation for what these artists go through, put up with and believe in. I certainly have.

Dax-Devlon Ross
New York City
October 2006

INTRODUCTION

If you've picked up this book hoping to become the next American Idol you might as well put it down now. If you think you're too good—too talented—to be selling your music on the street then I have only one question for you: Does anybody know who you are? Don't get me wrong, it's essential to have confidence in your abilities, but a lot of us are superstars in our own mind when the more immediate concern should be whether we're earning a living or not. Frankly, I didn't write *The Underdog's Manifesto* in order to teach you how to become the next pop-star. That's not my area of expertise. I wrote this book to show you how to survive as a working artist. In it I pass along the selling strategies that have worked for me and share some of the experiences that have helped shape me as an artist and entrepreneur. If you let me I might even help you get out of the job that's sucking the creative life out of you every day. Believe me, I know how hard it is to work 50 hours a week at a job you can't stand and still try to make music and be there for your family and have some kind of a personal life. That shit is hard. It's damn near impossible, in fact. But what if you could make the same amount money (or better) through your music? Wouldn't your whole viewpoint on life change? Wouldn't your spirit be more at ease? I work and live off my music. I pay my bills off my music. And I wrote *The Underdog Manifesto* so you can do the same.

Of course, I'm assuming you have some talent to begin with. If you don't then I can't tell you what to do. I'm not trying to be mean; that's just real talk. If you're "whack" then anything I say is going to be null and void. So, my second message is that you have to understand if your product is good. Contrary to what you might've heard, selling CDs on the street is not like selling drugs on the block. There's a world of difference. I put my heart and soul into my music because I know when people buy my album they trust that I'm giving them something quality.

You might be wondering, "Who is Creature anyway? What does he know?" To put it bluntly I'm a black man in America who's dedicated most of his life to making music. God gave me that gift. I'm a Master of Communications, a Master of Ceremonies, a Musical Conveyor conveying my thoughts to Masses—whatever you want to call it. But I'm also a human being *before* I'm an MC. By that I mean I gotta eat, keep a roof over my head and have some money put away for a rainy day just like anyone else. For a long time music wasn't giving me what I needed to survive; for a long time I was just like you probably are right now: frustrated. There's nothing worse than having a quality product and continually getting the runaround. After a while, the rejection, the false-promises, the bull-shit politics, the industry bureaucracy—it all eats away at you. I don't have to tell you what happens once the demons start to infiltrate your mind.

I was damn near homeless when I started meeting guys like Percee P., Logan P. McCoy from The Third Message, and Duo Live—independent artists making their living on the streets of New York. They were the cats who inspired me. If there was a show, they were there selling CDs, even if they had to pay to get in. If they could get on the mike, then they would make the most of the opportunity. They were constantly investing in themselves, constantly taking inventory, constantly figuring out ways to improve the quality of their craft and reach a wider audience. Watching them earn their living on the streets showed me where I had gone wrong in my thinking. See, I was so focused on getting signed by a record label that I had completely overlooked the other option available to me: doing it myself. Those cats inspired me to get my product together and hustle like I've never hustled before. Three years later I've sold thousands of CDs, started my own record label, signed my own artists, put money away, done shows around the country, built a strong, faithful following, been written about in the likes of *The Village Voice* and *The New York Times*, and featured on Starz and MTV. What's funny is that the last thing I was thinking about when I started selling my music on the streets was the publicity I'd receive. I was thinking about putting some money in my pocket and getting my music out there. That's all. I even had a reporter once ask me what I planned to do if I didn't blow up. I looked at her like she was crazy.

"Blow up?" I said. "What do you mean 'Blow up?' I make a living off my music now! I'm blowing up already. Anything else is just upgrading."

The mentality of that reporter is the mentality of most people, though. Most people think there's only one way to make it, especially in hip-hop, where everyone says the main goal is to be signed by a major label. I grew up with kids who were straight dope on the mike but they haven't been heard by the public yet because they're living by what the mainstream market Says is "hot." They're still trying to conform to what they think people will like. They're still hoping they'll "Blow up." What they haven't realized is that a lot of people are famous and still broke. I'm not stuck on being famous anymore. My views—the views I'm going to share with you throughout this book—are a lot more realistic. For one, you can't be worried about what other people are doing. You've got to make your own lane and worry about what you're doing. You can't change every year to be somebody else. You can take inventory of what people like and don't like. But everybody isn't going to like what you do and you gotta be cool with that. At the same time I guarantee there are fans out there for you being you. It's just your job to find them, and the only way that's going to happen is if you get out there and let them know you exist. The days of sending your shit to some A&R are coming to a close. If anything that's a gamble, a long shot. Me, I don't gamble and I don't bet on long shots. I'd rather put my life on it.

I honestly believe you can take control of your career too. I wouldn't bother writing this book otherwise. But you have to be willing to put in the work. That's lesson number one. You have to treat this like any other career. You're only going to get out of it what you put in. It's easy to come out when the weather's nice. It's easy to come out two days a week. That shit ain't nuthin'. That's the safest way to go. It's when you can come out when it's freezing, when it's nasty outside and your bones hurt—*and still make money*—that you know you've stepped onto a higher plateau. I'm not going to lie to you. People will act up. They will say a lot of fucked up, fly shit. When people are having a bad day you will feel it. The question is how will you deal? Will you take it personally? Or will you hold your head and keep your cool so the next potential customer doesn't slip by? In this game that's what separates the amateurs and the pros. In this book I'll share with you my survival secrets because I want you to see my come-up. Keep in mind, I didn't write *Underdog* so you could rush through it and go right back to what you were doing before. I wrote it to challenge and transform you.

Before we begin this journey together I have just one more thing to say. A lot of us give up before we ever give ourselves a shot. Because our careers aren't taking flight like we expected them to, we throw in the towel. I sincerely believe that you can survive as an artist if you're determined. I'm a living example of a blue-collar MC. I represent a renaissance of working artists who just want to be heard and make an honest living, cats who if the commercial world decided today that hip-hop is no longer a valuable entity will still be doing it. I'm definitely not the only one who could write this book. There are a lot of us grinding in these streets. I just happen to be the one who decided to put our story in print.

I.
FRUSTRATED AS HELL

Certain days you never forget. Certain days stay with you, haunt you—they become life-markers. You involuntarily use them to check your progress, or lack thereof. For me December 10, 2004 was one of those days. My plane landed back on American soil and just like that, the party was over, finished, kaput. After a month on the road—after a month touring in Europe for Christ Sake—I was home, again, New York fuckin' City. The absolute last place on earth I wanted to be.

A couple of months earlier Mike Ladd had called me and asked me if I wanted to go to Europe for a few weeks. It was going to be me, him, Rob Sonic, Beans and Bus Driver. We were going to hit up Ireland, Amsterdam, Spain, Scotland, Belgium, Germany, France and England. At first I told him I needed to think about it. I was still working off and on, on my album. I had already been shopping the EP. At that point I was just trying to do my own shit. It was Creature or Bust. If it didn't work out this time I was going to give it up. It was only after thinking about it for a couple of days and talking to people whose opinion I trusted that I came to my senses. The tour was scheduled to begin on my birthday. If there was ever a definitive sign that I was doing what I was supposed to be doing this was it! I'd be starting a new year doing what I loved to do and getting paid for it. It was a beautiful thing. I even remember the first time someone asked me what I was doing for my birthday. I said, "I'm going to fuckin' Europe."

The tour was amazing, everything you can imagine a tour being. For that period of time, the guys you're on tour with become your family. Mike and I had been old drinking buddies from way back. We'd both been sober for a little while so we were like each other's support. Rob I knew for fuckin' ever. I had toured with Beans before. He and I got close during the tour. I met Bus on the tour. He and I became cool too. He wound up doing a cut on my LP the next year.

The road is not real life though. I don't care if you're making a lot of money or a little. It's not real life; it's condensed life. You're going through real things but it's not the same thing as waking up and going to a job, paying your bills, dealing with your family issues. For that month, and even though I was like the low person on the totem pole, I was catered to. Wherever we went there were handlers and their whole job was to make sure we were comfortable. Then there were groupies—guys and girls— who just want to be around you because of your talent. So when I got off the plane—it was me, Rob and Beans—the shit exploded. Right away I was thinking, "Damn. I'm going back to shit, going back to sleeping on my sister's couch." Yeah, I had a couple bucks in my pocket—a couple grand—and I had sold a bunch of CDs and had some great experiences, but the fact of the matter was I didn't know where to go from there.

I think what really fucked my head up when we landed at JFK was that I was the only one going back to a job. Those other guys were living off their music. They were returning home for a while to hustle for a minute; then get

2

back out on the road. They weren't going back to a job. For me it was back to the grind. As a matter of fact, the shock of being back inside real life was so sudden and difficult that I didn't even go back to work right away. I couldn't. I took another month off. Everyday I just went to movies and hung out. I didn't want to be a part of this world. I would go to the library, check my e-mail, go to the movies then find someplace to chill for a whole month. I wouldn't even go home. I was trying to keep that high rolling along by doing light shit. I wanted to be in another world as much as possible.

I really got into music when I was a sophomore in high school. I was supposed to have gone to John Adams to play football. I was a helluva football player. But before I was supposed to start Michael Griffith was killed in Howard Beach. That was a big deal back in the late eighties. After my guidance counselor talked me out of going to Adams I enrolled at Frances Lewis in Fresh Meadows. The school was in a predominately white neighborhood but the student body was multi-ethnic. We lived on 107th, so I took the 7 train to 111th then hopped on either the 17 or 27 bus. In total it was about a forty-five minute commute. There were kids from all over the place in school with me. The only problem was that the school didn't have a football team. I was stunned when I found out. My guidance counselor had assured me there was a team. Turned out she had tricked me. With my football career over I turned my interest to music. I had always been into all kinds of music. My pops did whatever it took to bring money into the household. He had day jobs in advertising and real estate but at night he used to sell music. He'd take my brother and me out with him. We'd be all over New York selling Soul and Blues tapes. We'd be in barbershops, bars, post-offices— wherever. Those were my first experiences selling and that was as early as '85.

So, I grew up surrounded by all kinds of music. My favorite shit back in the day was RUN DMC's *Raising Hell* album. I also liked Public Enemy too. But then on the flip-side I was into groups like Twisted Sister and Quiet Riot. Back in the day—before cable television—channel 68 used to show all kinds of videos. One minute they'd be playing "King of Rock" and the next they were playing Metal Health. In fact, the first high school band I put together was a hardcore rock band. We called ourselves Short Notice. Even then the plan was always to figure out a way to fuse hip-hop and rock. We wanted to be like Bad Brains with Rakim on the mike. This was back in '89.

By '91 I had formed a group called Triflicts. There were three of us: me, my man Buck, and Gab Gacha. Buck doesn't even do music anymore. He just writes. Gab just got home from a ten-year bid. Meeting him introduced me to a whole other world. He showed me a side of Corona I hadn't seen growing up: the street. Growing up I had always been into playing sports. With Gab I was in the streets rhyming, in the streets hanging out, in the streets drinking. I had never really done that shit prior to that. That was an important stage in my life. In many ways it's made me who I am today. I introduced Gab to Buck, who I had known since '88 and had been in my original hardcore band with. We all just vibed. Even when we got together we had a vision. We knew it was going to take three years to get to a level where we were ready to be signed and sure enough in '94 we got a deal. At first, Fever/Def Jam was interested in us. But then our manager took us to Island Records and they signed us on the spot.

To be honest, I didn't feel any different after we signed our first deal. If anything it felt like prophecy. We always said it was going to take three years to get a deal and three

4

years later the deal was on the table. It was a single deal with an option for an album. After everybody got their cut the three of us walked away with $333. The thing was I didn't even care about the money. I was just on some rap shit. I played ball all night, got drunk, tripped on acid and wrote raps and chased girls. That was my life. I wasn't working. I was living with my parents. I'd be at Rob's house tripping all fuckin' day with my man Skila. Back then Rob's place was like a rest haven for stray artists. We all hung out there. People would be in and out all the time. Then at night we'd get fresh and go look for girls. I was a bum for hip-hop but I was going to blow up.

We recorded a song called "I'm Terror" but the record company balked when it came time to clear the sample. We were using a line from Ol Dirty Bastard's "Brooklyn Zoo", which was still hot at the time. The record company said ODB wanted like $2,000 for the sample. Not a lot of money. But the record company wanted us to pay for it. It didn't make sense. We went through a couple of months going back and forth with the label. Then we started having problems with the kid who did the beat. He wanted more money, a guarantee that he would produce a certain number of songs on the album—all types of shit. We wound up doing the beat over again only to have the record company come back to us and say they were ready to pay for the sample. By then we were fed up. We told the label to go screw themselves. The single never came out and the label, ultimately, let us go. I didn't even really sweat it. My attitude was like, "Fuck it, we'll get another deal." I went back to writing rhymes and looking for girls.

After the Island deal fell through, our manager, JB introduced us to the Beatnuts. He grew up with JuJu, plus they were from Corona and at the time we were reppin' Corona hard. In '96 we put out the single *Genuine* with

Don't Make Try on the B Side for Hydra Records. The Beatnuts did our production. Pretty soon were doing shows with them. We were supposed to be the group they were going to bring out. Everything was going to happen. But then that shit got fucked up too. Hydra Entertainment—our label—said we were going to do a video. That didn't happen. Then they made other promises that weren't kept. The label of course had excuses. They said that the single started off well but then it slowed down. Then they said it was doing well in Japan. "Why are we here then?" I said. "Take us to the Japan. Let's go get the yen." I was twenty-two at the time and I'm telling the label what they needed to do in order to promote their investment. That's when I realized a lot of executives in this business are idiots.

JB wanted us to put our album out ourselves but the independent scene wasn't happening in New York. In the Bay Area you had cats selling their own product, but in New York it was still about getting that deal. So we weren't keen on the idea. We wanted everyone to hear our music. We didn't just want our people and a few others hearing it. It got weird after that. First Buck got tired of the business and stopped rhyming. Then the Beatnuts started to be more interested in Gab. They wanted him to go solo. They were going to put out a single with him on one cut and me on the other. I wasn't feeling that idea. Not to take anything away from my partners, but I had started the group. I was writing the hooks. I was the one writing the concepts for the songs we recorded. I had even come up with the group name. I decided to make it easy for them. *I* broke the group up.

In one respect I felt that Triflicts had run its course. We had too many of the wrong people around us to get where we needed to get creatively. Too often we were competing to outshine one another rather than focusing our energy on creating good songs. Plus, I was starting to run with a whole new crew of cats. My man Frank "Ceams" Arrieta[1] had introduced me to Rob in '94. In turn, Rob introduced me to DJ Jun (who now goes by Preservation) and to Fred Ones, the producers behind Sonic Sum's first two albums. Meeting Fred was huge for me. At that time I was rhyming all over other people's albums but because I didn't have any money for studio time, I wasn't producing my own material. Fred gave me his space to make music for free. He respected my flow enough and believed in me enough to invest that time and energy in me. He's a huge reason *Never Say Die* was recorded. Fred is also just a special guy. He gets along with everyone. If he doesn't like you then you must be a real muthafucka. I met Mike Ladd around this time too. He was also an important piece to the puzzle for me. He had already released *Easy Listening for Armageddon* and had made a name for himself on the underground/indie scene happening downtown. Every week he was performing somewhere. After he did seven or eight of his songs he'd call me up on the stage and we'd just have a freestyle session.

The downtown scene was popping in the late '90s and early '00s. Cats would be on the mike every night. There was always a show somewhere: The Wetlands, Brownie's, The Cooler, Baby Jupiter. I remember Fred and Jun had a residency at Spoon's. We'd all go there and listen to music and drink. I was already a maniac on drinking, a few of us were. In many ways drinking became my life. I still rapped. Still did shows. Drinking just became a part of it. The thing

---

[1] In 1998 Ceams leapt to his death from a building. It was a blow to us all. Nevertheless, his passing would be instrumental in Rob taking his career to the next level and putting out *Sanity Annex in 1999 and Plaster Man* in 2002.

is, not drinking I have a personality. I'm kind of abrasive, some might say aggressive. Something that I would let fly sober, I wouldn't let fly drinking. Shit that I know I would keep to myself sober, I would address when I was drinking. It was a hard period for me. You have to keep in mind, by then I'd already had a deal. I had worked with the Beatnuts; I was on an album with the X-Ecutioners. So when I was drunk I'd go up to dudes and tell them straight up, "You're whack. Why do people like you?" Obnoxious shit, really. But, see, I knew in the back of my mind that I had to make this shit work and it wasn't working the way I had planned. I was still living with family, still waiting to blow up. I still didn't have a job. When it came to money, I always seemed to get by. I'd do a gig here, a gig there. Basically I was scratching and surviving—we all were. You have to understand something, though. It was a lot more communal back then. We would pool our resources however we could to get by because music was what lived for.

I thought I didn't have to work, frankly. I was going to be an MC, what the fuck did I need a job for. Then I moved in with my man Skila. I've always been fortunate enough to have people in my life that looked out for me. They seemed to see things in me that even I didn't see. Skila was another one of those people. When I didn't have a place to go, he opened his apartment to me. He really showed me what work ethic was all about. Don't get me wrong, my dad had worked hard all his life. But this cat would stay up until five am making a beat and still get up in time to make it to work by ten. We had some serious conversations about where my life was headed. Fuck my career as a rapper. At the end of the day, I wasn't even ready to receive blessings because I had yet to humble myself. Ironically, it took me getting out into the blue-collar workforce to begin developing my artistry. Over a stretch of six years (roughly

8

'98-'04) I took on a series of jobs just to pay the rent. I was a messenger, a rigger, a dishwasher. When I worked construction I'd come home after twelve hours of back-breaking labor and just pass the fuck out. I must've had at least three different supermarket jobs. Actually, those were some of the best jobs I had. I could always steal food to eat.

For a minute, life just got really, really real. People I was close to were getting locked up or killed. I was desperately trying to keep my career alive. The one good thing was that I was always only responsible for me. If I was suffering, I was suffering, not my wife and kids.

The other thing about living with Skila was that he introduced me to a new level of my artistry. I had grown up in New York City. All I knew was spitting lyrics about how dope I was. Even if my girl had just dumped me and I was heartbroken, I would still rhyme about fuckin' some bitch in the bathroom. In the mid '90s you could go anywhere and catch a cipher. It wasn't just battling either. It was like, "Yo, let me hear something." Next thing you know you'd be with two people you don't even know free styling. Then two more kids would come. Then it's seven of you. Then it's twenty and everyone is just going. You always knew where you were at lyrically. There was no illusion. And the goal was to get as nice as possible. You wanted people to say, "Damn, that muthafucka's nice." It was sport. You don't get on the basketball court for people to be like, "Oh his shorts look good." You get on the court for people to be like, "That muthafucka's shootin' the shit out of that ball. He's dunking that shit something nasty."

But, see, New York will also get you caught up with the Joneses. You'll mess around and be the ballplayer who can only dunk. The rest of your game will suck because you neglected it. Living with Skila was crucial in that it showed me what I wanted to become as an artist. I had been

9

listening to Outkast since their first album came out in '94, Goodie Mob since '95. I had been listening to Public Enemy before that. I always wanted to write about real shit. I wanted to be honest about myself and about the things I was going through. It just never appeared in my work. In a way Skila showed me how to do that.

So, artistically, the late '90s were integral to my development. I was meeting all types of new cats, being exposed to different audiences, different venues, different sounds. I was working hard for the first time in my life. In the process I went from being a straight lyricist to a writer. The music I started writing began to reflect that. In 2000 I released an EP entitled *De Ja Taboo Graphic Art* which was really the culmination of that entire period of growth in my life. Most of the songs had been written a year or two earlier, and for the first time I was proud of the quality of the music rather than just the niceness of my flow. With that album I was able to show my vulnerability for the first time.

Despite the creative strides I was making, I still had a drinking problem. Fuck it, I was an alcoholic. We're talking finishing bottles in a club. I hit rock bottom one night at the APT, a trendy club in the Meatpacking District. I was in the basement with my man Kukoo getting tore up. I'm laughing at dudes, making fun of them, talking all types of shit. I didn't like the way they were carrying themselves. They were pretending to be tougher than they were. So I called one of them on it. Then I just punched the kid in his face and started laughing. Needless to say I got myself arrested. You would've thought that would be enough but it wasn't. Even at the precinct I'm wilin' out. I'm cursing at the cops. I'm screaming. They could've brought me up on assault, disorderly conduct—all types of charges—but they let me go once I sobered up. Basically an hour after I walked into the precinct, I walked out.

You would think a close call would sober me up. Uh-uh. Not me. It took watching my nephew for a few days to sober up. From the time he was born my nephew and I have been close. His father has never been around so I've always taken a fatherly role in his life. He was still in diapers at that time. Honestly, it wasn't even a major decision for me. I just could never drink around him. Suddenly one day became two days and two became six. Next thing I knew I was twelve days sober. That was it for me. September 12, 2002 was the last time I had drink. And just like that, I saw my life begin to improve dramatically. I sold a couple hooks. I made guest appearances on MF Doom's *Vaudeville Villain* album. In '03 I went on my first tour. But after doing music for nearly fifteen years, I still wasn't living off it. I was starting to wonder if I ever would.

II.
WAKE UP
AND SMELL THE HUSTLE!

I had a lot of time to look back on those years during my month-long hiatus from reality. Only then did it dawn on me how important they had been. That month was actually an essential phase, in retrospect. It allowed me to get my mind in place. It was prepping me to make some kind of move, though I still didn't know what it would be. It allowed me to walk the streets and sit on trains and in movie theaters and just ask myself some hard questions. How long was I going to keep blaming people for my lack of success? How long was I going to keep depending on someone else to do what I needed to get done? How long? When Mike asked me to go on tour I was going to give up music. I was working at a telemarketing firm. I didn't know where my rap career was going. It sure as hell wasn't going in the direction I needed it to be going in. I was starting to think about what I was going to do. The tour had resurrected my career for all intents and purposes. It was my job to run with that momentum.

Without even thinking about it all that deeply, I started cutting dead weight; dead weight in my head and the dead people around me. Thoughts that weren't helping me grow and people who just weren't on the same page as me anymore. Once that dead weight was gone I didn't have those excuses anymore. I couldn't say my album wasn't done because such and such forgot to do X,Y, and Z. Finally I was ready to deal with the situation. Yeah, I had shopped my record. But I hadn't given myself a real chance. Not a real one. I hadn't taken it to the streets. This shit started in the streets and I hadn't taken it there. I had watched 50 Cent resurrect his career through the streets. This guy was left for dead and little by little he brought himself back to life. From getting shot to a month later putting out a song called Fuck You, and sounding totally different, having a whole different swagger. The next thing you know for the next two years he was strangling muthafuckas like, "I'm here and I'm not letting go until you die and I live." 50 has a very different thing going on than I do, but that mentality inspired me.

Then I got inspired by Bus Driver. His success was tangible in a way that 50's wasn't. Sure I knew Rob and Mike and Beans better but something about meeting a complete outsider who was making his living off his music affected me profoundly. Bus had been part of Project Blowed out in Los Angeles. He'd been on the scene out there for years. But there were people who knew me that didn't know him. Sure, sometimes he had a hard time making his rent, but he always did. Instead of going the commercial route, he'd spent ten years doing him. His success showed me that if you keep doing what you're doing and just get progressively better, you're going to pick up more people. You might never blow up but you're going to keep growing. But if you stop, you're dead. You lose that momentum. The key was to keep productive. Write the song. Do the song. Perform the song. Get back to work.

So I looked at 50 and I looked at Bus and I asked

myself what I really wanted. Yeah, I wanted to sell a lot of records like 50 but I couldn't do that. Even when I stripped all the bullshit away, I just wanted to live off my music anyway and get my music to the people. I couldn't say that I'd given either of those goals a real shot. Yeah, I had shopped my stuff to people but the indie labels I was approaching didn't want to put my record out. They didn't think I was quirky enough. I had to understand that indie labels tend to make music in their own liking. A major might do something they don't necessarily like but that's going to be the next thing to blow up. An indie label is all about putting out the shit they like. All I saw was this garbage being put out. I just knew my shit was way better. In reality I couldn't be mad at them. I'd never given myself a real chance. The shit started in the streets and I hadn't taken it there. Seeing Bus showed me I could do that. I could sell. I wasn't twenty-one anymore, but I was still young enough to have the energy, the tenacity. Bus, and to a lesser extent 50, created the atmosphere for me to say, "Fuck this. I'm going make this happen."

So there I was down to my last $100. I thought I had no choice but to go back to telemarketing. The hours weren't necessarily bad. I was cool with the manager. I came and went as I pleased for the most part. That was why I had the job in the first place. But when it came time to return to work I couldn't even stomach the thought. I was done working for people, through being miserable for no good reason. I respected the grind; I just didn't want to be a part of that particular one anymore. When the day that I was supposed to go back in came I just didn't go. I didn't call. I didn't resign. I just didn't show up. I was done. I had put my life into music. Now it was time to get paid off it. Giving up was just not an option.

I still had about eighty CDs left over from the tour. I

gathered a bunch of them up and hopped on the train. I got off at West 4th and headed to Fat Beats. Officially, it was my first day at my new job working for myself. From then on I was going to be on the grind everyday. I'll never forget that first sale. I managed to get this guy to stop long enough to give him my independent music spiel. At the end of it he said, "Fine. How much are they?"

"Seven," I said. There were only seven songs on the EP so it worked out to a buck a song.

He only had a ten, though, and I didn't even have change. He handed me the money and just as I was about to run and get change for him he stopped me.

"Never take less than ten," he said and walked off.

That shit shocked me. I liken that to the moment when the rain finally stopped. It was still wet outside, but I could see the sun out that bitch and it felt like I hadn't seen it in forever.

The hardest part about coming out, for me, was getting back into the mentality of talking to strangers. On the road I would talk to people so it wasn't exactly new. The only difference was that I was going up to people and making them aware of me as opposed to coming off stage and having people already know who I was. When you're performing people can see what you're capable of. They can see if they like you. Chances are they're going to buy your album anyway just because they just saw you on stage. That's how people are. But, see, when you're really ready to make money that overcomes whatever trepidation you might have about approaching someone you don't know. That's that determination, that hunger. That's what has to override everything in your mind that's saying, "This ain't gonna work."

What surprised me early on was that I got such a positive response from people. A big part of that was having Slug from Atmosphere (*Better Man*) and Jin from the Ruff Ryders (*Whut u Know Bout Me*) on the EP. People knew those names so immediately I gained credibility in their eyes. What's funny is that I never intended on having any collaborations on the album. All the collaborations just kind of happened by accident. I was trying to get Slug to put my album out on Rhymesayers. It was his idea for us to do a song together instead. After I met him a couple of times, I sent him four or five beats and he chose which one he wanted to rhyme over. He was supposed to come to New York to record it but he wound up recording his lyrics in Minneapolis, which was still cool. Jin and I go back. In the early '00s I was spending a lot of time out in Yonkers at the Ruff Ryders studio just trying to be heard. Me and Jin got cool and I ended up doing a hook on his first album. In return he spit a verse on my album. Between those two cats alone I was attracting a more diverse crowd, and I didn't even know it or think about it like that at the time.

Getting out on the streets wasn't just about money. It was about rebuilding my confidence, reigniting my fire. From 2000 to 2004 I had been on at least one album every year that was in stores. Two of those albums were considered significant underground records: Rob's *Telicatessen* which came out on **Def Jux** in 2004 and MF Doom's *Victor Vaugn-Vaudeville Villain* came out on **Sound Ink** in 2003. To be totally honest, that was some shit I didn't exactly want to do. But they paid me and I did it. The next thing I knew people were coming up to me on the street asking if I was the same Creature from the Doom album. I didn't realize it but I was on the scene.

So, for me, hitting the streets saved my career. I went from wanting to give it all up to realizing I had a body of work that people were aware of and respected. That gave me a springboard. I wasn't just anybody. But even a little bit of a reputation can only get you but so far. I still had to figure out what worked, and work it. As the days became weeks and the weeks became months that's exactly what I did.

The first thing you have to understand is that this is a profession that involves a lot of psychology. You gotta have a clear mind so that you can read other people. It's like chess in a way; you have to think your moves through beforehand *and* on the spot. Otherwise you will not succeed as an independent artist. Let me give you an example of what I mean. Say I see a guy walking down the street wearing a Dallas Cowboys jersey. Right away I know something about him. Maybe he borrowed the jersey but chances are he's a fan, if not of the Cowboys then of football in general. I know football, so I'll say something like, "Do it for Ed 'Too Tall' Jones! Do it for Drew Pearson!" An obscure reference to the Cowboys of old will trigger in his head. I can only know that if I actually grew up watching the Cowboys myself. More often than not it'll make him slow down or smile or respond—either way I've got my in. I haven't sold him yet, but I read him and in some way catered to him, which most people like.

I've boiled down the most essential lessons I learned when I first began selling my music independently. Notice that they're all broad enough for you to apply them however you see fit. But if you put them to use I promise that you will experience more success than you have in the past.

Be Observant: This is extremely important. As I just pointed above with the example I provided, by being observant you can modify your approach to each customer. Sometimes you need to be more aggressive. For instance, if I see a kid wearing a Black Star t-shirt, then I know he listens to underground hip-hop. I know I can approach him as an underground artist. He wouldn't expect anything less, in fact. At the same time, if I see someone, say a woman in her fifties or sixties, I won't approach her the same way. For one, I know that's what she's probably expecting. I can throw her completely off by finessing her rather than putting the pressure on her. Think of it this way. You might be an ill-ass dunker, but you can't always slam it home every time. Sometimes, you have to shoot the lay-up or the fifteen-footer. Remember, the objective is to score, not necessarily look good doing so. This might sound simple, but it never ceases to surprise me how many cats I know who don't know how to observe their customer and modify their approach accordingly.

Find a Connection: I can't stress enough how important it is to find a point of connection with people. You only have a small window of time so you have to read people quickly and find an entry point before they get away. It might be something as simple as complimenting a woman who's dressed nicely or telling a guy that he reminds you of someone you know. I actually made a sale that way once. I told a guy he looked like someone I grew up with. He in turn asked me what school I went to. As it turned out we'd both graduated from Francis Lewis. That kind of stuff makes people feel good. It makes their day. You get to talking about this and that and the next thing you know you've got a sale.

Bring All Experience to the Table: I'm never being phony when I tell people I listened to Motorhead or the Ramones growing up. I loved these bands as much as I loved A Tribe Called Quest and RUN DMC. They were a part of my childhood. Everything that I show people is me.

I'm just a complex person with a lot of experiences that in other settings doesn't get a chance to come out. In this business, all the things that I was ostracized for growing up, being well-read, listening to various forms of music, having different types of friends, I rely upon these things on the streets. It's what sets me apart from a lot of other artists. Honestly, my having knowledge that they wouldn't expect me to have helps them get past the exterior sometimes. It helps them see beyond the stereotypes and all the judgments they normally make without even realizing it.

Be a Master Communicator: A lot of people can't speak. They're not good communicators. They beat people in the head, they come off angry, they stumble and stutter; they talk too much. I see it all the time. It's important to practice your pitch. Whatever you say, say it clearly. Even though you're going to modify your approach and find a unique connection, once you get the potential customer to stop, it's time to sell. I'm going to touch on this again below, but it's important for the pitch to be succinct. With me it's a very simple spiel. "You look like an open-minded person. Check out my album. I did it myself, fourteen songs all independently produced. It's socially conscious." Notice I don't put a price tag on the album nor do I mention exactly what type of music I'm making. There's good reason for that. I'll explain both of those rationales below.

Make NO Assumptions About People: A lot of people market themselves to a particular type of music, I understand that. When you go into a record store or a bookstore or any other store that sells commercial art, you find certain products under certain categories. The amazing thing about selling music independently is that you're not a slave to the corporate structure. You simply have to understand what that means and how deeply we've all been brainwashed to think inside the box. My personal philosophy is simple: everyone is a potential customer, everyone. If you live in an environment that's artist friendly you'll be surprised by who buys your record; one minute it can be a sixty-year old woman, the next a twelve-year old kid. They both might get something out of it. But if you assume the sixty-year old doesn't want to hear it then you've lost that chance.

On another note, some people are what I call "donation freaks." By that I mean if I ask for a reasonable donation they might give me even more than I would've asked. Strange as it may seem, some people just like giving money away. I might approach them and the first thing they'll say to me is "I don't want to buy anything." But if I say something like, "I'm not even selling it. I'm only looking for a reasonable donation to support independent art," they might change their whole tune. It's all in the wording and how you make the customer feel. If they feel like they're giving to a good cause then so be it.

Keep it Light: people respond to charisma. Let me say that again: people respond to charisma. But what is charisma? It's being outgoing. It's being engaging. It's keeping a positive attitude. It sounds cliché but on the street being positive is crucial. There's a way to keep a smile on your face without grinning and shucking, which you'll never catch me doing. By keeping that smile people feel that lightness. They want to support it. I joke a lot. I tell a lot of jokes. For real, hearing NO a thousand times a day is not human. It's not. But we're not doing shit that the average person is doing. I don't take it personally. I keep in mind that people have hard days, hard lives. A lot of people don't like themselves or what they do for a living. Any number of things could've happened the moment before they ran into you so you have to keep that in my mind at all times. There's an opportunity there as well, an opportunity to help brighten someone's day. That's got to be part of the job. I'm not just making money. I genuinely like people and that's crucial. If I didn't like people then I would've failed at this a long time ago.

Put Yourself in the Buyer's Shoes: If there's one thing I can't stand it's when someone calls me and I know they want a favor or to borrow some money, but they keep beating around the bush. That annoys me. If you live in a major city chances are people's time is precious. They don't have time to hear you give them a five-minute song and dance. Think about it from their perspective. What can you say that would captivate them in the briefest period of time? Efficiency is the goal. It's the same way with the music and with the stage performance. On another note, make sure your breath is fresh. The last thing you want is to be up in somebody's face with bad breath. You might think this is a joke but I've seen it happen and it isn't pretty.

Rebuttals. Rebuttals. Rebuttals: Most of my sales come from people who say "no" before they say "yes." The fact is most people don't buy right away. A lot of people say, "I'm okay." My response is, "Hold on Mr. Okay let's talk about this for a moment." Again, think on your toes keep it light and be persistent without being a pest. Some rebuttals will become standard, but you're always going to have people who are just a bit cleverer than you expected so it's important to be, again, light and prepared for whatever comes your way. Some people just want you to work for the sale. There's nothing wrong with a little work.

Avoid the "Hip-Hop" Label: No, that isn't a typo. I hear guys saying stuff like, "Support real hip-hop," all the time, and I generally avoid them. There are a couple of reasons why. First of all there are too many negative connotations attached to hip-hop. For a lot of people the word hip-hop is an immediate turn-off. Granted most of these people don't know what they're talking about, but that's not the point. The point is nothing you can say will change their mind once they've got it in their mind you're selling hip-hop, which brings me to the second reason I avoid the term hip-hop. It backs you into a corner too quickly. You disarm yourself before the battle even begins. Instead of referring to my music as hip-hop, I refer to it as independent music or grassroots music or something of that nature. There's a huge difference in the connotation, not to mention in the response people usually have. One thing you have to understand is that there are a lot of people in the world who want to support independent music. They want it to stay alive because they believe it's important. And it is. It's a way for people to be heard. It's a way to indirectly stick it to major media companies. It's a way to maintain some integrity in a consumer society. I love hip-hop, but I've learned that the way to make money is by avoiding the term until you've made the connection. Once you've made the all important connection and the buyer sees that, "hey, this guy is okay;" chances are he or she will give the music a chance because they like you.

These were the basic laws that I learned to live by my first few months out on the streets. They were vital. After one month I had earned enough to put down a security deposit and first month's rent on my own apartment. I decided to wait until June in order to move, but when I did I had more money than I had ever had in my life. I saw myself change radically and dramatically. I was at peace with myself. I didn't feel the need to make excuses anymore. I felt like I honestly didn't need a record label. I became more responsible than I had ever been. My rent was paid on time. My bills were always up to date. I became disciplined in my spending habits. I stayed sober. I started eating better. It was amazing: I wanted to live, to thrive, to succeed. I damn sure didn't want to be broke again. I liked having money in my pocket, money in the bank. I liked being in charge of myself. If I ever felt the lazy bug on my shoulder all I had to do was remember being down to my last $100. That was motivation in and of itself. That just wasn't going to happen again. That isn't going to happen again. I'm passed that stage of my life. I fucked up enough already. However, just by being successful at what I love I've learned that as much as you fuck up, you can always get back up and walk again.

Interlude #1:
Re-cap

Questions to Ask Yourself

Who in my life do I find inspirational?
_____

Why?
_____
_____
_____

What can I learn from their successes?
    1.
    2.
    3.

What is my favorite excuse?
_____
_____
_____

What can I do to take that excuse out of the picture?
_____
_____
_____

What do I really want to achieve?
_____
_____
_____

Knowing what I want, have I given myself a real shot to have it?

_____

_____

_____

If I could describe it, what would a real shot even look like?

_____

_____

_____

Self-Evaluation
Identify Your Dead Weight.For example, mine were:
1. Associations with people who weren't on the same page.
2. Alcohol: I was a lush.
3. Ego: Seeing myself as being too good for work and entitled to stardom.

Make your own, honest list of three.
1.
2.
3.

Key Points to Remember

The difference between *tangible* examples of success and *intangible* examples is crucial. For instance, if I had relied solely on 50 Cent as my model for making it, I might've never hit the street. But knowing Bus Driver and Beans and many other cats and seeing them survive off their art gave me the belief that I could as well. We need tangible examples in our lives to succeed.

Nobody owes you anything. It isn't about what people should and shouldn't do. If people decide to help you along the way that's great, if not, do it yourself.

Maintain momentum. The key is not letting up the gas. Once you've got things moving, keep them moving. Don't stop to admire your progress.

Interlude #2:
the Rhyme Inspector Percee P.

Profile

Quotable: "If you give up rapping because you don't have a deal then you're not a real MC."

Intelligence: Percee has been rhyming since 1979 when he was 10. He's considered a living legend that's yet to get his due. He released his first single on **Big Beat** in 1992. He was awarded the coveted Source's Rhyme of the Month. Has rhymed with Big Daddy Kane, Lord Finesse, Nas, Big L, Pharoah Monch, Kook Keith, Wildchild, Aesop Rock, Jurassic-Five, Jay-Lib, Madlib, C-Rayz Walz and others; gained legendary status for his years of independent grinding on the streets of New York. In 2003 Percee signed with **Stone's Throw Records**. His first album, *Perseverance*, is being produced by Madlib.

Stomping Grounds: Born in the Bronx, worked the downtown scene (*Fat Beats*) for years. Now based in Southern California but still grinding in the Valley.

Selected Discography:
Put It On The Line (Ox Remix/BX Remix) *12" single*
Legendary Status *CD comp 2005 (MTA)*
The One And Only: Greatest Hits *LP (bootleg)*
Nowhere Near Simple *12" single 1996 (Vmax)*
Percee P. & Ekim - Lung Collapsing Lyrics *12" single 1992 (Big Beat)*
Top Priority (Percee P. & D-Nique) - Let the Homicides Begin *from "BQ In Full Effect" 12" EP 1988 (Gotham City)*

Visit http://members.aol.com/ProfQuater/Percee_P.html for complete list of Percee's work
Website: http://www.stonesthrow.com/perceep/

29

Developing your strategy

Everything is a strategy. I figured I had to do something that was going to promote me and I wasn't the type that was going to labels with demos. I wanted to be in one spot so people would know where to find me. I wanted my music to branch outside the hood and I knew the downtown area is where a multitude of different races congregate. I knew whoever went to Fat Beats was more likely to know more than just commercial artists. They'd be more knowledgeable about these underground artists and these independent labels that have been around for years but just haven't made big names for themselves. I also knew at Fat Beats they'd at least have some of my earlier work, which meant I could direct people to my stuff in the store.

Once I started putting out my tapes and CDs I watched the music start spreading. People started writing stuff about me on their own and posting it on the Internet. I started seeing pictures of myself online. Then I started collaborating with other artists. Then people started actually coming to meet me. Cats started hanging around me. I became that dude in front of Fat Beats. It benefited me. It made me realize that whatever you're doing there's always people watching you. And I realized that what I was doing was inspirational to others who also wanted to get their music out there.

At the same time I didn't just stand in front of Fat Beats. When the store closed I'd hit any event that had a bunch of people together in hip-hop: open mikes, SOB's, Irving Plaza, *Zulu Nation Anniversary, Rock Steady Anniversary*. Anything hip-hop—I'm still a fan—I was going over there with whatever I had left from the day. Even if I had to pay to get in I'd pay because it was a promotional thing. I'd bring my music with me and move product while people were standing in line waiting to get in. I'd go up and down the line. My strategy was to get the first of the first people and have less to sell once I was inside. That way I could focus more on meeting other artists inside. If people meet me and like me enough they might want to do a song with me and that'll create some money right there. By the time I came out I wanted to have nothing left at all. That's my goal: to leave with nothing.

I'd do the same thing at Rock Steady Anniversary. They have thousands of people in line waiting to get in. I'm just going up and down the line selling. "Percy P. Percy P." Everywhere I went I put my name out there so even if you'd never heard me spit, you heard of me. I made almost a thousand dollars at Rock the Bells (annual hip-hop festival), this year and last. I do it all day. From 12 pm to 12 am I'm out there. No rest. I come early to get it started. I'm out there promoting. Out of all those thousands you're bound to find 'em. It's my job to find 'em. Tomorrow, I'm not working at such and such. I may make it look easy and good, but to me this is my life. This is it for me. Everything I'm doing is survival mode. I come with drinks so I don't have to stand in line. I get a bag with wheels on it. I'm on it. People from all over come to these events and I want my stuff to go back with them.

Self-Confidence

In order to make others believe in you, you have to believe in yourself. It's not that I'm bragging but it's kind of like a pimp. The way he talks to himself, that's the way he's going to get a female to get behind him or to want to work for him or advocate whatever he's trying to push. You really have to make people into hardcore fans so that when they walk away they feel something special about

31

you. So you have to ask yourself what is it that's going to make you stand out from the others. I always come out looking clean in a nice outfit. Appearance is important. If they've never heard of you but you're looking decent, looking good, they'll all of a sudden give you the time of day. People realize if you look good then you must be serious. You gotta look the part to make it. I believe in living up to the hype.

I used to bring pictures of myself from shows with other artists that I've made music with. I'd bring CD covers and put them inside photo books for people to see my body of work. I'd bring them flyers to show them who I've performed with. I show them that just because I'm standing there it doesn't mean I'm not doing anything further so they can respect what I'm doing. I'm educating people on Percee P. and who better to do that than me? So while I'm selling product I give them my history. I tell them that I got quotable rhyme of the month in the Source in '92. Matter fact it was the first song Big L was on. I can tell 'em I've recorded with Lord Finesse. I can tell them that I brought Ultra Magnetic to Stretch Armstrong, that I brought AG to Stretch Armstrong. I can say these things because it's true.

Perseverance

You have a lot of dudes that look down snobbishly on dudes like me on the street, walking past with a nasty look. Some dudes are cocky enough to fan you away. That's part of our history, though. Our people, it's sad to say, have to be co-signed by white folks in order to be validated. We lack self-knowledge and the industry is designed never to celebrate our history. No other music does this to their artists. Hip-hop is the only genre that says once you're 30 you can't be in the game no more. That's messed up. Why would you erase somebody who's got history to offer the game? Why would you tell Kool Herc he's too old to be a DJ when he's the one who started it? A lot of it's depressing and you're always in a position to snap and lose your cool, but you have to make people comfortable enough to get them to stop. Some people ask me how I do it. It's something that comes. The more you do it the more comfortable you become with doing it. A lot of people don't know how to deal with rejection. You can't get mad. You have to consider your reputation and the game itself. You can't jeopardize the whole independent scene. You gotta think about everyone. My advice is to give them a card. Give them a website. Let them see for themselves. Then they'll come back.

We do this because we want to and because we don't want to resort to having to settle for doing shit just to get a deal. I feel like if I can't do it the way I want to do it then I may as well stand on the street and sell my shit. **Stone's Throw** recognizes and respects what I'm doing. They're gonna let me continue to do what I'm doing but they're going to help me take it to another level, which is happening. People respect the label. The label has fans. The more fame I get, the easier it is to capitalize so I feel like saying I'm down with them is a good thing. They are trying to do things that are different. At the same time it's making it easier to sell my own independent work. I'm doing shows but I still come out on the street because I realize there're still mad people that don't know me. I'm always going to promote myself even with a deal. That shows the label that you're behind your product. I'm not going to stop doing whatever has gotten me where I'm at now. I've sacrificed a lot for my music. God tested me too long. I feel as though I had to prove how much I really love hip-hop. He gave me periods of my career where I had success. He put me in contact with other artists. He validated me. I firmly believe God tests those before he rewards you because He wants to see where your heart is at.

III.
ARTISTPRENEUR WITHIN

I first heard the term artistpreneur three years ago when in Chicago doing a show. A manager by the name of Commander put me on to what it means. You're more than just an average artist. An artispreneur is a go-getter. An artist sits around and waits for someone to put them on. They're paid to perform a certain task. If they're not told what to do then they're stuck. An artistpreneur is the general. It's his situation. He takes full responsibility. He sees the bigger picture, whatever that may be. At the same time he's his own best soldier. For example, say I gotta press up a thousand CDs. The businessman in me will hustle up the twelve or thirteen hundred it's going to cost to pay for the job, pick the CDs up, store them, then come back out and sell them. And that's not even the half of what an artistpreneur does.

As an independent businessman/artist it's your job,your duty,to know about any event that's related to your music, even if you don't like performers, even if you think their shit. is whack, you need to know about it. Again we're talking about getting past the ego because the only person you're hurting by not going to an in-store event or to a performance by an artist that shares your fan base is you. Even if you're not selling at these events, you're promoting. You're handing out flyers. You're shaking people's hands. You're building and nurturing relationships that may help you down the line. You're branding yourself. People always ask me how I know about so many things happening and I tell them point blank that my livelihood depends on it. Most of the time, I like to know about events well in advance. That gives me time to prepare, particularly if the event is out of state. That way it's my decision. An artistpreneur avoids making hasty decisions whenever possible. For one thing, the less time you have to prepare, the more money you're likely to have to spend and the more likely it is that something important is going to be overlooked. I personally like to weigh my decisions out: how much is it going to cost to get to the event? Where will I stay when I get there? If I spend three hundred dollars and wind up making a thousand, then it's worth it. At the same time, I might spend three hundred and only make three hundred but it might be worth it if I make the right connections. In the case of a local event that draws one thousand people I might sell only 10 CDs, but that's still $100, not to mention the fact that ten more people who didn't know me before now own my CD and know my name. And that's all at a minimal cost.

Believe me there have plenty of events that I would've rather not gone to. A lot of times I'd rather be in the studio, at home chillin', kickin' it with a shorty. But when I decided to come out and take my career seriously, I meant that. That wasn't just sunny day lip-service. All I have to do is remember hitting rock-bottom. Remember being sick and tired of being sick and tired. Remember all the excuses I was making

36

for so long. Then I think about how far I've already come. That's all. For me, taking my career seriously means working harder for myself than I've ever worked for someone else. Just think of how many people you know that give their lifeblood to a job that only gives them a paltry check in return. Imagine if they put even half of the energy they put into making someone else wealthy into themselves. If you don't have the discipline to put yourself first then there's just no way you can succeed at this.

Plus, in the larger scheme of things, going to these events is a small sacrifice. I like what I do for the most part. A lot of people can't say that. I really don't even see it as a job. Being an artist and an entrepreneur allows me to more completely express all that I am capable of. There's no disconnect between Sadiq and Creature. People may know me by a stage name, but I'm always myself. And that self is a social being. I like interacting with people on a daily basis. Frankly, any performer who doesn't, I have to question what they're doing in this line of business.

A big problem with the way the recording industry is set up now is that too many aspiring artists think they're too good at what they do to be bothered with the business side of music. They say to themselves, "I'm talented. Why should I have to sell my CDs? Why should I have to hand out flyers? Somebody else should be doing that." They watch these shows on television and they see these "successful" people who have street teams and they think that's how it's supposed to be. Street teams are all well and good, but if you're just starting out you're not going to have one. So what do you do? You have two options. Complain that no one knows who you are. Or become your own street team. One of my man Shake-O Blaize's favorite sayings is that it's easy to say you're great when you're your own fan. I don't know about you but I'm not going to buy a thousand copies of my own CD. I know guys who've recorded more songs than ten Tupacs. They're in the studio like animals. They might even be more talented than I am. But they don't bring their music to the people. They'll press up CDs and give them away to their friends! What kind of shit is that? They always complain about being broke and yet they're giving their blood, sweat and tears away! What that tells me is that they don't believe in their product to push it. They sincerely don't believe. They're afraid of succeeding because it's one thing to talk about what you want to do and another to actually do it. There's pressure. There's expectation. There's the possibility of failing. Instead of facing it, they're content to be stars in their own minds. That's enough for them. That's not enough for an artistpreneur, and it shouldn't be enough for you.

What you have to keep in mind is that there's nothing wrong with hustling. There's no shame in the blue-collar grind. An artistpreneur doesn't even indulge that type of defeatist thinking because he knows it's based on misguided beliefs perpetuated by consummate critics who rely on excuses for their own failure. Just because you're out hustling off your music doesn't mean you're any less talented than someone with a recording contract. We all have to start somewhere. At one point even the most popular muthafucka was a "nobody." Essentially there are three ways of getting a record deal with a major label. One is by creating a buzz on the streets. Two is by piggybacking off an established artist. Three is by selling units on your own or through a boutique label.

I simply can't say enough about how important it is to invest in you. Beyond anything else, your mind set changes when you throw down $1,300 for a 1,000 CDs. Originally my EP was only supposed to be for promotional use on tour and to shop labels with. I wasn't even thinking of it as a fundraising tool for my LP. It was only after I got back off tour and I still had CDs left over that it dawned on me that I could use the money from the EP to finish the LP, and that's what I did. Now, I'm not saying you should hustle up the capital if someone is willing to front it to you. If you can get it done quicker then so be it. But always keep in mind the sense that no one did it for you, that no one can sit back and congratulate themselves on your success because you went out and got it. That's priceless. It confirms your belief in yourself and in the quality of your product. It makes everything a little more real. It lets the people around you, even the people who support you, know that you're serious.

At this point I should say a few words about the company I started shortly before *Never Say Die* was released, **Coffee Grind Media**. Five years ago I organized a team called Insomniac Dream. There was a group of us. We were all friends independent of the music we were trying to make together. But there were too many people in the kitchen. I couldn't make the right recipe with it. Everyone wanted to be the top chef. Everyone wanted their dish on the menu. To put it bluntly, it didn't work. Personal loyalties aside, I had to put myself in the position that I was comfortable with. While shopping the EP I had the chance to see the ins and outs of various labels. An important lesson came out of that experience even though I didn't get a deal.

No one can do me better than I can do me. A record company may have been able to put money into me, but they were never going to have the same drive that I had, nor were they going to have the same long-term vision. That was the clincher. It was time to start my own company. I had always wanted to anyway. I wanted to create something that was me. That I liked. I didn't want anyone else telling me they were going to put my shit out two years down the road. Fuck that.

Practically speaking I had three options for setting up the company. Option one was a sole proprietorship. Option two was a corporation. Option three was a limited liability company.

Sole Proprietorship:
Benefits: This is the simplest form of business. The owner has total management and control over the company. There are no significant formalities to setting up a sole proprietorship. The owner can sell the business at their pleasure.

Drawbacks: The owner is personally liable for the company, thus placing his or her entire personal assets and wealth at risk. If an owner is married, that owner puts the community property at risk.

Corporation:
Benefits: A corporation which is properly formed and operated as a corporation assumes a separate legal and tax life distinct from its shareholders. A corporation pays taxes at corporate income tax rates and files corporate tax forms each year. Corporations can offer fringe benefits to employees. Corporations enjoy many constitutional protections.

Drawbacks: There are a number of formalities that a corporation must adhere to. These formalities include extensive maintenance of records, formal meeting requirements, issuance of shares to shareholders, and maintenance of adequate capital in order to meet any "foreseeable" business debts. Failure to follow these formalities can result in the shareholders being held personally liable for company debts under the "Alter Ego" test.

Limited Liability Company:

Benefits: Like limited partnerships and corporations, an LLC is recognized as a separate legal entity from its "members." This means only the LLC is responsible for the company's debts thus shielding the members from individual liability. An LLC's failure to hold meetings of members or managers is not usually considered grounds for imposing the "Alter Ego" doctrine, where the LLC's Articles of Organization or Operating Agreement do not expressly require such meetings.

Drawbacks: Filing of an Operating Agreement with the state.

After weighing my options choosing to set my company up as an LLC just made sense. It gave me the protection without placing all the burdensome demands of the traditional corporate structure. The cost for filing was $600. Four-hundred dollars went directly to pay for incorporating the company. Two-hundred dollars went to the requisite filings with the state. Before I go any further I should point out that I didn't do this right away. I don't recommend anyone spending $600 to incorporate when no one even knows who you are. You've got time to build your foundation. I waited nearly a year, and even then I used money that I received from a video game I did a song for to pay the fees.

But that's really only the surface story to the whole

purpose of incorporating my company. Setting up Coffee Grind was another mental milestone. It was a further investment in me, another confirmation of my mission. I chose the name because it represented me. I'm grinding and that's the image I want to portray. I actually got the name from something Rob said in one of his songs back in 2000: "It's just my daily coffee grind." My philosophy is that the name should represent you because it's going to be what people identify you with. If I'm Gangstakilla Records and that doesn't represent me people are going to be like, "Why you calling yourself that?" The name shouldn't be something you're not comfortable representing. At the same time, you have to keep in mind the overall purpose, which in my case is to create a brand that sticks in people's minds.

Incorporating the company was also significant because it made me consider how I was conducting myself as a businessman. Put another way, it helped me get everything on the same page. I started seeing myself as the representative of my company, a company I depended on for my livelihood. These may seem like idle gestures, but the accumulation of tiny steps makes for a huge transformation. I don't know if it was by osmosis or what but I began to reflect the sense of urgency depicted on the Coffee Grind logo. It helped me solidify my pitch too. Every company needs a pitch and the pitch should play to its strengths. Shelling out that money and going through that process forced me to look into the meaning of my message and to the means by which I wanted it conveyed. Coffee Grind represents a blue-collar work ethic. It represents a sense of social awareness. It represents the streets in a certain aspect. But it also represents humor, which is evidenced in the company's play on words. I'm not killing anybody, nor am I talking about cars or bitches on the corner. That's not what I'm about. It ain't. I'm about everyday life. Depending on whom the buyer is I'll say it's introspective because I know they'll relate. To someone else I might have to break it down and say, simply, "I'm talking about my life." But, either way, the message is consistent and it relates back to the mission of the company.

In the process of switching my mind set and my lifestyle to that of an artistpreneur I learned a few key lessons about blending the business with the art. Apply them and get your hustle on.

- ☐ **Quality Product**: This alone sets the precedent. It's the most important piece to the puzzle. It doesn't matter how nice you are as a salesman. That'll only get you so far. After a while people are going to know your product is whack and word *will* spread.

- ☐ **Market Research #2:** Choose the right place to get your CDs pressed up. Talk to other people. Your basic interests are numbers and quality, consistent quality. Despite the widespread accessibility of internet companies, my personal preference is to pay the company a personal visit. That's important to me. People need to see a face. A face creates a connection. They take a little more responsibility for the work. You also know if someone is bullshitting you. I've heard horror stories. People do shaky work. They don't do work on time. They sometimes forget they're not doing you any favors, that hard-earned money is being spent for a service that needs to be done appropriately.

- ☐ **Build Relationships**: This relates back to what I said about attending as many events as possible. People often ask me how I get shows. Well, it's pretty simple. I'm always around music. If I'm at a show, I'll ask who books the shows and why I'm not performing. I hear people crying about there being no shows all the time. Maybe there aren't the shows you want to do, but there are shows. Maybe they don't pay the good money, but they are still shows. Once again it's time to be the artistpreneur. Promote the show. Get people out. That's your job.

☐ **Market Research #2**: Shows are an invaluable way to get real-time **feedback**. Instead of dreaming about what people think you're actually hearing what people think. Use the opportunity to find out what they like and why. That's market research in its truest form. There's no buffer. No one telling your manager you're whack and then telling you they really liked it. It's cut and dry in the street.

☐ **Re-invest**: I made sure the money I earned from the EP went back into the LP. Once the LP came out people saw where their money had gone. The shit was professional in every aspect. It was my way of thanking people for the support they gave me. People need to see progress otherwise they start to question your word. Progress doesn't necessarily mean walking around with a chain or having a car. It means upgrading.

☐ **Momentum**: There have been times I've sold all my CDs by five o'clock. Now, there might be a show that evening. I have a choice. I could say, "Fuck it, I've made enough money," or I can go home and get more CDs. If it's coming fast you have to ride the wave. If you have momentum you have to go with that. That's just business sense. There's going to be fast days and slow days in every business, that's why they say prepare for the rainy days.

When you're doing better than you usually do, go harder. There's more money to be made. More people who don't have your album. It's up to you.

- **Don't Count the Numbers**: Some days I don't get my first sale until three o'clock. For real, some days you make a hundred bucks in ten minutes. Whether it's fast or slow you have to stay out. The easiest way to do that is by not counting who says yes and who says no. I like to think of it this way. Say I get a thousand no's and ten yes's. That's a hundred bucks.

- **Shaking Things Up**: It's good to make your presence felt in different areas. It's a big world. Say you're in San Francisco. You're on Market. You want people to know you there, but then there may be somewhere like Fillmore where people support music too. It's important not to just be that guy who sells in one place. By the same token, if there's nothing happening in front of one location you also don't want to beat a dead horse. I always say give it an hour, but you also have to know the energy. You have to know when to walk. Once you start walking you might run into someone, make a few dollars, then you come back three or four hours later and boom! The dead spot is hot.

- **Keep it Light**: I try to always have fun. I never forget that I'm working, but there's a way to keep it lighthearted. It helps keep things positive and fresh. The point is to make money and enjoy life.

- **Make Your Lifestyle Work for You**: Too many people are working to support their lifestyle rather than making their lifestyle work for them. Me, I like to go to shows, sell music and talk to girls. I know what I like so I incorporate it into my life. I'm never on the clock, but I'm never off the clock either. Some people like to smoke weed. Well then make time for that. Get up early. Take a puff. Reset the alarm and for the next hour or so do whatever.

☐ **Create a Schedule**: Even if you don't write it down, it's important to give yourself a routine. I'm up everyday by ten or eleven, but that's because I don't get home until three or four in the morning most nights. By one I'm out on the street. That's a good time to start because people are into the flow of their day. It wouldn't even make sense for me to be out early in the morning. People aren't in the right mind state to buy music on their way to work. After a few hours, three or four, I check my e-mail, visit my MySpace page. I correspond with people. Send out messages. Post bulletins, whatever I need to do. Then it's back to work for three or four more hours. At night there's always an in-store event or a show. Wherever I go I have my CD. I might be talking to people, hanging out, but I'm still working, still making money.

☐ **Be Firm**: As a general rule I don't like to drop the price of my CDs but everything depends on the person and on the situation. If I think you really are interested and just don't have the money then I'll work with you. I've had people buy it for $5 and come back to give me $5 because they liked it that much. By the same token, if I think you're just trying to get one over, then I'll walk. Even as an artistpreneur you have to keep in mind that people can't go into Tower or Virgin and ask to pay $5 for a $15 CD. I know what my work is worth. When you're not a fly-by-nighter you don't care as much either. Some people devalue the game by underpricing the product. They'll sell ten songs for $3. That's crack head shit. I'm a businessman. I'm hustling; they're getting change in a cup.

☐ **Say a Hustler's Prayer**: Create a ritual for yourself. Everyday before I leave the house I say a prayer. You never know what might happen out on the streets so it's important to give thanks and to ask for blessings and to get your mind prepared for the day ahead.

Interlude #3: "Lucky"
Logan P. McCoy

Profile

Quotable: "The first time I ever sold a CD I had just quit my job. I had no source of income. Because I didn't have any other options, I had to make money. That was my motivation."

Intelligence: Pioneer of the street hustle. Co-founder of **The 3rd Message, Inc**. Twelve CDs released since the summer of 2001. Developed unique, forward looking sales strategy whereby T3M only released fifty-five hundred copies of a given album, the idea being to create a catalogue of music that can be re-released at a later time. Over 60,000 units sold on the street to date. First independent hip-hop label to have a fully functional digital distribution system.

> **Stomping Grounds**: NYC
> **Discography**:
> **A Compilation** (2001)
> **The 3rd Message: 2nd Mission** (2001)
> **The Unexpected** (2001)
> **A Hustler's Guide to Prosperity** (2002)
> **Drive** (2002)
> **Brain Candy** (2003)
> **Year of the Under Dogs** (2003)
> **Power of Suggestion 1** (2004)
> **Good Luck** (2004)
> **Power of Suggestion II** (2005)
> **Failure is Not an Option** (2005)
> **www.t3m.us** (2006)
> **Website**: www.t3m.us

More than an MC

When I first came out of high school in 1994, I worked in corporate America for a little bit. I was also enrolled in college. I was supposed to become a mechanical engineer. But that just was not what I was trying to do. I had been doing music prior to that but something just clicked in me to try to do something with it, so when I got a deal with a small independent label I abandoned all those things that I was doing as far as my education, career, all those things. I put them to the back burner just to pursue this thing called music. I didn't realize what a self-revelatory journey it would be. My partner and I compare it to martial arts all the time because it's an art form. The more respect and love and honor you pay this art form the more it pays you back. But the dividends are so subtle that you don't realize it until you look back. That's what happened with me. In doing the music I've had to assume many different roles just to realize a dream. When I started I wasn't making beats. I was just a straight MC. I wanted to write more rhymes than Solomon. That's all I wanted to do. You're getting ideas that you never knew were there and yet they're coming from you. Then you gotta go back and relearn these same ideas that generated from you. So there's something mystical about that. And just that whole mystery being revealed was intriguing enough to keep me doing it.

I eventually had to buy myself out of that first deal. It was crazy but that was how I started learning about what really made the business move. I started to think about society at large. You can have a revolution but without economics it's really pointless. That's what made us become entrepreneurs. When we first started to sell the music on the streets in 1999 I had seen other people do it, but I had noticed a lot of people couldn't be consistent. The consistency factor was what was missing. In recognizing this I realized this is a business and if you can't generate enough income to put out another project then you're done. That's when I really started to take it seriously that we could be something. In the beginning we didn't even accept the fact that we were entrepreneurs. We used to downplay that because at the end of the day we saw ourselves only as artists. Our original goal wasn't even money. We went out with the mentality to share our music and garner an audience. Lacking the business foresight we didn't even think, after you garner an audience what are you trying to do? But then I realized that there are people like Miles Davis who are still artistic and very astute at business. That's what made him successful. The world does not always recognize the most talented artist; it recognizes the best-selling artist. We wanted people to hear our music and to keep ownership of it. Those are the reasons we were out there on the street. I didn't do this so I could be underground and have only five people hear it. In realizing that, we decided to follow the entrepreneurial spirit. We used to stand right in the door of Fat Beats. The hardest part was not was not hearing no, it was actually standing there when nobody was coming and you having to deal with your own demons inside telling you, "What are you doing? Why are you standing out here? Are you crazy?" It's almost like being in solitary confinement, mentally speaking at least. Being able to overcome that hump is the key because once you've lost it you're going home. As a salesperson, when you work on commission you don't eat when you don't sell. We used to stand out there and not use the bathroom until every CD was sold. It turns out you can do it. You can flip it. Just doing that helped us realize that we had something because the response that we got from our audience made me realize that people really do want this kind of music. That also was great market research because I got to speak to people from all walks of life and they told me their qualms with hip-hop and how it wasn't speaking to them. It gave me an angle in the quest to reach these people and believe it or not just like wearing those hats made me learn more about myself; I learned that I was really a businessman. I started to look at my past prior to me making music and I realized that I've always been a businessman, I just didn't realize it. Coupling that with the art is what has brought me to this point. It's helped me see the potential where others don't.

Business is just the relationships that exist between people. That's really what business is. If you look at real entrepreneurs a lot of them don't have the so-called traditional training that real students have as far as being disciplined about reading, writing, etc., to be successful. And yet they have this uncanny ability to see talent and tap it and bring the best out of people; that in and of it is a talent that most people don't have. I learned that on the streets. I had to talk to strangers. I had to take the abuse from strangers. I learned how to be a salesman. Now I can parlay that into a resume that looks impressive because our company really is a company. I can use that to go work for a legit corporation.

I started as just a rapper. I didn't know anything about contracts. I didn't know anything about anything. Now we're working toward being those entrepreneurs that built these Fortune Five Hundred companies. Who says that can't be a reality tomorrow? Why can't we have this kind of economic power? That's what T3M is all about. At the end of the day we were able to put out 13 CDs because of ideas we had in our head without leaving the house. We have CDs in Europe without ever leaving America. This process itself has made me realize that the potential is inherent within us as human beings. I believe there's a force that we don't understand that guides us in every single day of our lives. And I believe it's that same force that communicates to us in the writings. I'm not the same person when I started. I've been transformed. The music did that.

IV.
STREET INTERVIEW
7-12-06
NY, NY

Broadway and 23rd Street

Key:
    Q=Dax
    A=Creature

Q: Say I'm an artist who's curious about coming out on the street. What's the first thing you'd tell me if I came to you for advice?

A: I'm assuming you have a product already, something that's done. I'm assuming you've already got your product pressed up and it's ready to go. With that in mind, you have to want to be out here. That's the first thing. If you don't want to be out here, no matter what I say it's not going to help you. If you really hate it, I mean really detest it, your work is going to suffer as with anything. You have to have your mind in the game, otherwise why come out? I learned that lesson the hard way.

Q: How so?

A: I want the good for people so much that I've put them into positions that they shouldn't have been in. See, if you're not really grinding at the level I'm grinding at then it doesn't help me to help you grind. I end up losing steam. I've tried to help talented people get started in the past. Brought them out here and tried to teach them the ropes only to lose money. I've lost money because of someone else not wanting to be out here. Talent is a beautiful thing. Talent without being active is just potential tragedy. The thing about being independent is that you don't have the time to develop people. You need that momentum.

Now I know that if I don't meet you grinding then I'm not going to deal with you. It's not about being mad at them. I'm just not going to be associated with you. I'm on another page. We might even be in the same book, I'm just another chapter. I just want to come out.

Q: That reminds me of when we spoke the other day. It was raining outside and yet you were still on the street.

A: We were still out here making good money. It started off gloomy but real warm. As Shake-O likes to say, "The weather was being disrespectful." We ate lunch. Then we wound up walking to Broadway because it looked like it was going to rain and we knew we could stand under the scaffold if it did. Things started off slow, real slow. Traffic was light. Then it just started raining money. First it was one sale; then another, then this dude paid me, Shake-O and Unknown fifteen dollars a piece for our records. By five I had over a hundred bucks. The rain got heavy for a while so we laid low until it died back down and came back out again. This time I made another fifty.

Q: What's that about?

A: It's the confidence of knowing there's going to be a better day. Sometimes it's frustrating. You gotta chalk up a bad outing and forget about it. If you carry everything that happens with you it's going to affect you. But these are things you have no control over so why grieve about them? I can control coming out here. As unpredictable as it is, I know that if I come out even my bad days will be better than some people's good days. I can't rely on people writing about me. If it happens I'm grateful but I can't rely on it.

Q: So you've told me that I have to want to grind in order to be successful out here. What's the next thing I need to know?

A: NO is the first step to YES. You're going to hear NO so accept it. The more you hear NO eventually you're going to hear YES. People are so scared of hearing NO that it stops them from moving forward. They don't even get in the game. It's safe that way. You can convince yourself that it won't work. I got into an argument about this yesterday. These cats I know have recorded two albums worth of material and don't even have an inkling of how they're going to put it out. Studio stuff is one of the easiest things to do once you get the gist of it. But you need money to put it out. I asked them where they planned on getting the money. Were they going to max out credit cards? Were they going to ask their parents? Even if they had told me they planned on working overtime at the job, that would've been a plan. They didn't have a plan. It's a little delusional to record albums with no idea how to get them in people's hands, don't you think? You're going to hear it. So what? NO. NO. NO. Then somebody will say, "Yeah, let me see what you're working with."

Q: It seems as though what's made you successful is your attitude towards people in general.

A: Everyone takes things so personal. I can tolerate someone unless they're insanely jerky. You're skin's gotta get thicker. You're going to deal with different personalities. I always keep my mind on the bigger picture: Why am I out here? I'm out here to advance my career. That means putting my music into people's hands. That also means getting better shows. For example, maybe you meet someone who's a little obnoxious. They're not really doing anything to deliberately offend you but they're just an asshole.

But this is the person who books better shows. I need to talk to that person. My job is to find a way to block that obnoxiousness out and get the better shows. It's that simple. All of this, "I like; I don't like" nonsense is irrelevant. You don't have to like someone in order to conduct beneficial business with them. Some people won't hear me but understand why your career is at a standstill.

Q: A moment ago you spoke about knowing why you're out here. I'd like you to go into greater detail on that subject because it strikes me as the foundation of the daily grind.

A: If it's not in the forefront of your mind, you lose track. It's like this: television, magazines, I don't do this for that, man. I do it to get money in my pocket, to get my message out there and to be responsible for myself. I know people who get easily distracted by the lifestyle, women, partying. You're your own boss out here. No one tells you not to get drunk when you're supposed to be working a club. No one tells you, you should be out here working; meanwhile you're leaving with a girl. I've known cats that will stop working and go chase after some girl. No discipline, none whatsoever. The minute a cute girl walks by they off the clock. Then a week later they're wondering why they're broke.

Q: For someone who's new to this, what does

"responsibility" look like?

A: There's a few different forms it can take out here. First off, the people who are successful out here generally don't cut corners. Cutting corners only comes back to haunt you in the end. My man has done a half-dozen different album covers for one album. Each time he gets a new shipment he throws together a new cover so he can get some quick money. Instead of investing to get them done respectably, he's left with a bunch of hasty covers that he's going to have to do over anyway because he knows they look cheap. That's wasted money and time.

I knew from being around Rob and Fred that I couldn't have my stuff looking crazy. You're already setting a certain standard when you do that. It can look independent and still be grimy, but it can't look crazy. It's got to look like a representation of the quality so that people can look at it and realize you're serious. I understand that sometimes you don't have the money to put into it, but you still have to have it looking as best as possible for that time. If you know that by waiting a couple of days you'll have a better looking product then you need to wait.

Another way people cut corners is by coming out without their songs being mixed. Their songs will be sounding crazy and then they have the nerve to get mad when people tell them about it. You shouldn't have cut that corner. It just means you have to go back to the studio and spend more money anyway. Moreover, you have to deal with people who've already heard the unmixed album. What are you going to tell them? It's good now? You shouldn't even hit the streets if you're stuff is not at a certain level, until your stuff sounds quality so that you can listen to it.

One thing you have to remember is that most people already have a preconceived notion about street stuff. They already think it's not as good because it's not in stores. They think you're a knock-off. I'm nobody's knock-off. You're stuff has to be quality in order to dispel that myth. If it isn't everyone suffers.

Q: What other forms does responsibility take?

A: I'm a firm believer that if you don't set deadlines then you're going to be idle. You'll never get things done. Goal setting is the key to success. You can't be aimless. You have to shoot with a target in mind. If you're aimless then there's no goal. You're never able to assess your progress or lack thereof.

Q: What's the biggest roadblock independent artists face?

A: Being dependent on favors. Obviously we all need them. But once you start depending on people to do stuff for you for free it gets done when they have the time. You could need it done yesterday and it won't matter. It kills you. I call it Homeboy Time. That gets thrown out the window with some money.

Q: Speaking of money, what is your advice for working the shows?

A: Know when and where they are. Then be there before the show starts. Be there while people are in line so you're catching them before they go in. Before they spend all that money on alcohol or whatever they're buying in the venue. They still have money in their pocket then. They can't tell you they've spent all their money. They're smoking a cigarette, talking, waiting around. They're not going anywhere. They're a captive audience. One thing you've gotta remember is they're going inside to see someone else and they've reserved that money to spend on them. You're the underdog. It's your job to beat the competition to the punch. Show starts at eight then you need to be there at seven. As soon as people start creeping you're like, "Oh, check out my record." You've got an hour. That's a lot of time. Then if you go inside yourself, you gotta work the crowd.

Q: Before we move on, what is one more form that responsibility takes?

A: Following through. Say I meet someone who could be beneficial to me. Instead of saying, "Yeah, yeah, I'll be in touch," actually do it. Call them. E-mail them. Remind them who you are and what you talked about. Not following through is the reason a lot of people are where they are. The door of opportunity opens up and they're high. No one says when opportunity arises. But if you're not even in the right mind state how are you going to even receive it. You gotta have your antennae up.

Q: When has following through worked for you?

A: I met the editor for Kool-Aid magazine out here on some "check out my album" shit. Once I found out he was with a magazine I gave him the record. But then I called him and asked if he'd listened to it. They turned around and reviewed the album. Once that came out I called him up again and suggested they do an article on me. Turned out they were thinking about the same thing. Now what would've happened if I had just left it alone? I got kids that have done reviews in different magazines that I don't even remember meeting out here. But once I see the review I make sure to call them and thank them. I let them know I'm grateful *and* that I'm available. You never know, maybe they've got something going on that I can be a part of. Keep relationships open so that when things happen you're one of the people on their mind. A lot of people are doing this. The go-getters, the people that are 'bout it, them the people who get the opportunities.

Q: What about when people say there's no future on the streets?

A: I say don't worry about me. I'm going to be okay. I'm going to be good. Worry about yourself. I happen to do this and I happen to be good at it. But just like everything leads into something else, the skills I use out here I can translate to other fields. I'm not going to go so far afield. I won't try to be a doctor but I don't want to be a doctor. I'd be wasting my time. I have no interest in medicine. If I don't sell music I'll sell something else. I can sell houses. I'll sell shirts. I'll flip something. Whatever I have to do, I have to make money. I'm not going to be broke anymore. I refuse to be broke. I'll stay out on the street until I make some money. I won't go home.

Q: Why do you think that people question what you're doing?

A: Everyone doubts everything. People's minds operate as workers. They don't operate as thinkers and visionaries. People don't see the skill involved in this. They don't think there's any level of expertise involved. They think anyone can do it. You don't have to go to college to rap. You can be ten and rhyme. That makes it a free-for-all. Everybody thinks they're an expert. You know how many times I've had random people try to tell me where I should sell, how I should sell. I ask them point blank, "Have you ever sold music before? Have you ever sold anything before?" The answer is always no. "So how can you be a specialist?" I ask them. "Do you go into a hospital and tell a doctor how to operate? Do I come to your job and tell you how to do it? But you're going to tell me how to sell? Sell something first. In the meantime, I take my tips in cash."

Q: Do you see yourself as someone who is changing the

rules of the industry?

A: I'm helping change them. I'm certainly not changing them by myself. I'm part of a movement of people saying we can be free from the nonsense and do something we love. New York is behind in this game. As ahead of things as New Yorkers are otherwise, when it comes to getting free of the nonsense we're behind. We're just starting to catch up. My goal is to motivate people to get free from the bull. Free from working the same jobs they hate. Free from drowning in misery. I guess that makes me an optimist. Maybe I'm living in a bubble. I just really want people to be free. I want them to want more. New York is for rich people. America is for rich people. But if you can find a way to make your life livable, enjoyable, and not be broke then you're free. I don't care about money per se. Money is options. Money means not being homeless. Money is saying I can buy a house soon, that I can put out my records. I know I live in a capitalistic society so I'ma play ball. But I don't care about money. I've never had it to begin with. I don't love it and it don't love me. We're using each other. It's a user-friendly relationship.

V.
MAKING THE BRAND:
(A DISCOURSE ON INTEGRITY, AUTHENTICITY, HUMILITY AND CREATIVITY)

```
7-19-06
6th Avenue and 8th Street
New York City

Creature
Shake-O Blaize and Preachermann
Q=Dax
```

Q: Who are some of the people that you've patterned your career after?

Creature: That's really a two-part answer. There are people who I respect and admire for their artistry. Then there are artists who I respect and admire for their entrepreneurial spirit, their hunger.

Q: Let's start with the latter.

Creature: Too $hort, he's a bad muthafuckin' man. You gotta think about it. He's selling his stuff independently in the early eighties. When Run-DMC was blowing up, he was selling tapes. That's crazy. Five years ago I wasn't even thinking about selling my own music. I wanted to hook up with a major label that was going to make me bigger. $hort hopped on the bus and was all over the Bay Area selling tapes. He decided he was going to put his own shit out. He would find out what people in different areas liked, then he'd make a song specifically for them! He's that dude. The Bay Area period is a special place. They're light years ahead out there. Even the Black Panthers started in Oakland. Ideologically it might've stemmed from Chicago and New York, but they made it proactive.

Master P is another person whose spirit I respect. He was also in the Bay. He learned that independent hustle from them out there. He was in Richmond, California for years, soaking up all that game out there. He didn't even say New Orleans until after Tupac died. He went back down South and the first couple of years he was basing his image off of Tupac. Then he started being on some New Orleans shit.

Without Herc, Flash and Bam there's no hip-hop as a whole. But without those other cats there's no independent scene. Cats might've sold their tapes, but cats like $hort and P took it to another level and became businessmen.

Q: We've talked about this several times. Down South, out West: they've done the independent thing already. They've created a blueprint for getting a major deal. But the same thing hasn't happened here in New York. Why is that?

CR: Everything is here, that's why. It's the same reason why a lot of people who come to New York are more successful than native New Yorkers. They come with a purpose. They come because they know there are more opportunities here. You know how many people were more talented than Madonna during the time she was coming up?

She was living in Corona for a while, not far from where I grew up. This is a chick from Michigan! Just coming here took a lot of balls. She put herself in a position to win, though. She was determined to make it. New Yorkers sometimes get so caught up in the whole system that we can't get shit right.

Q: Why is that?

Shake-O: The reason why a lot of people don't go that extra mile is because of the ego. The ego kills you out here. People have these huge egos for no reason. The humility has to come from your heart. No matter what you do you should be humble. That's what's going to take you to the next level. The more humble you are, the more you understand what you need to do in order to be the artist that you want to be.

Preacher: I had an experience recently that flows along those same lines. I was doing a show one night but when I got there the manager wasn't around yet, so no one was there to greet me. No one knew who I was. So I'm just hanging around waiting. The bouncer comes up to me and tells me I need to stand aside. Mind you, I'm the marquee performer. But I don't give him any problems, nor do I announce myself, although I easily could have. Anyway, I go do my performance and at the end of the night the bouncer stops me. He explains to the club manager that when I got there earlier that evening I was just standing around like a regular Joe. Then I got on stage and blew it apart. But as soon as I got back off I was regular people again. I learned early on that the great ones are always the most humble and I try to pattern myself in that ilk.

CR: I got a story too. A couple of years ago these kids invited me to a music festival in Europe. They really wanted me to come out. But since they didn't have any money to pay for me to get out there I wound up not going.

I would've made money out there. I would've had a place to stay. But every time I've been to Europe it's been on someone else's dime. The idea of buying my own ticket was weird to me. I felt like less of an artist. What I've learned is that sometimes you have to accept the situation at hand and make the best of it. Next year I plan on getting a ticket and just going out to Europe for a month. I'm not waiting for someone to bring me out anymore. I'm going to get in contact with the people and set everything up myself. There's enough people I've met through the years that are over there. I know there'll be shows. I know I'll make my money. I'm not going to sit around and wait anymore. Fuck that. I didn't wait this year or last year so why am I going to go back to doing that now?

Here's the thing. When you have talent and you see people with marginal talent doing more it can bother you. That's natural. If I watched MTV I'd be depressed and not thinking about how I'm making a living, how I'm happy, how my music is getting out more. I wouldn't think about that because I would keep judging my success against who's out there. I can't think about that stuff. That's not my path right now. I have to continue being proactive.

SO: If you're going to be the artist that you want to be you're going to have to make sacrifices. That's life. It's either you sacrifice or you might as well kill yourself. 'Cause that's what you're doing if you sell-out.

PR: By the same token, and just to get back to the question you asked about people who I pattern my career after, I'd have to say Lenny Kravitz. Lenny held out to do the kind of music that he wanted to do. Granted he had a father that had the ends, but at the same time things could've happened for him earlier if he had been willing to compromise on this and on that. I feel that you only get one shot to come through the door so if you don't come through the way you want to come through it doesn't really matter. That whole "do it this way and then do it your way later" stuff is nonsense. Your way may never come.

SO: Creating a brand is hard work. Some people will tell you that if you don't have holes in your shoes you didn't do enough work. If your feet ain't bleeding, you ain't worked hard enough. When I first decided I wanted to be an artist I did the same things most artists do. You hear these other MCs saying you should get a book and a lawyer. These are the first two things you hear. Then you get the book and it's an industry book. Industry books say that if all else fails then you sell your record in the streets. What is all else fails? When do you get to that point? Meanwhile, if from the beginning you had gone ahead and come out and built a foundation there's no telling where you would be.

CR: I think that's a big thing too. When you build a foundation you don't have to worry about trying to make the radio song that will get you paid. Muthafuckas make radio songs that never get played on the radio! What kind of nonsense is that?! I already know that I have to be independent to do what I do. I'm not ready to bend over. Yeah, I'm a character, but I'm not a wind-up doll. It's a thin line. You entertain people so naturally you have to wonder if you're shuckin' and jivin'.

Q: That's an interesting point. And it leads me to another question I wanted to ask. How do you draw the line between who you are on stage and who you are in person? *Do* you draw a line?

SO: I think you should intertwine your life with your art. I think once you become an artist, you should be that, all day twenty-four hours a day you should make that person who you want to be. I never want to be a package. I never want to present myself in any other manner, like I'm an actor. When you're acting you become that character. When you're an artist you should simply be who you are.

PR: People like to latch on to things that are shiny. What's the line from *Shaka Zulu*? "How do you catch a monkey? Show him something shiny." That's the truth. But if you have an internal shine then even the blind will know where you're at. Personally I know what I give off. I stand out anyway. It's not even about the afro. There's no reason for me to do anything else. I dress down a lot. One of the comments I get whenever I perform is that people didn't know I could clean up so well. I don't believe I have to dress up for people everyday. If you can't see my shine then you're not ready to see it. I have the utmost confidence in myself. I've already done things that will never be recorded by MTV or any newspaper. I've changed people's lives. I've helped people. But I don't hold up billboards saying that you need to accept me because my name is Preacher. Most people aspire to be accepted. I aspire to be great. If I miss greatness then I'm still good.

CR: I agree. I don't put make-up on. Sometimes I go from selling CDs to doing a show. If I can I'll stay home and get in my right mode. I'm performing all day. It's not like Superman appears all of a sudden. I'm Superman all day. I'm Clark Kent all day. People relate to real people. As simple as that sounds when you're approachable, sometimes it throws people off, but generally in our line of work that means a whole lot to people; signing an autograph for somebody, taking a picture with somebody. Chubb Rock said it best back in the day: "Sign an autograph you might make a new friend/ I never try to play the superstar that's mellow/ 'cause when these kids don't buy our records we'll be has beens/ and plus naked/ So we owe them, pull out your pen, sign an autograph you might make a new friend." Come on! If people don't buy your shit you're nobody. I'm not delusional about this. I have talent but if people don't support us there's no art being done.

It's necessary to be with the people, to be of the people. Creating a presence is essential. It's like air. You can't survive without that. A presence is when you go to everything involving something you're involved with—shows, parties. Shaking people's hands: "You don't know me, my name is Creature. Check out my album." It's going to people's communities. It's networking with people. It's collaborating with people. That shit gets around. Next thing you know somebody comes up to you and is like, "I was in Texas and you're name came up." Mike Ladd came back from France one time and was like, "this kid came up to me and was talking about you. He said he bought your CD in New York." People appreciate that you're real people.

Q: How have you been creative in marketing yourself?

SO: Self-promotion is the key to success. I do t-shirts. I do hats. I do stickers. I do twelve-inch albums. That way my music gets heard in the clubs, in the streets, at house parties—they still go on you know. The DJ in the projects who's throwing the speakers in the window and thumping your shit for you, that matters. Being creative is using what's at your disposal. If I can't make it on the radio I gotta at least be present on the streets. People actually forget about the streets. Actually Hot Ninety-Seven is not that big of a station. Don't get me wrong, it's major. But it's only one station. You can go to the independent stations. You can go to public stations. You can go to the college stations. They'll play you. By being outside you get to meet students who have radio shows. Some of these stations can be heard as far away as Ohio. That's enough to get you out there. It's not an overnight thing. You're putting in work. Everyday you're building, adding new listeners. If you're on a radio station somebody new is hearing you and every listener counts.

CR: Being digital is vital. This is a computer age right now. It's like a lung. If someone might not have the money to buy your album on the spot you have to have some other way for them to interact with you. Right now *MySpace* is vital. By the end of next year it might be shit. But right now, today, *MySpace* knocks everything out the box. I don't want to be pumping Rupert Murdoch but it's free. It's simple. It levels the playing field. You get a chance to break through with people who have a bigger fan base than you. If a muthafucka got a million friends you can connect with them and get them interested in your page, in what you're doing. You might get a bunch of pages just listing your event. You might get people who stop through and just listen to your music.

SO: It's the same thing that we're doing out here all day. It's another way of doing it. You're meeting people, but online.

CR: It's good to have your own website too.

SO: You don't own *MySpace* either so tomorrow that could be shut down or they could start charging.

Q: What are some of the things a website should communicate?

CR: A web page should be about you. What your music is about, new music, new shows, new collaborations; whatever it is. People want to know. They're you're supporters—I don't like calling them fans—and they want to know what you're up to.

Q: How would you advise someone just getting in the game to go about setting up their site?

SO: The more you know how to do, the more you can do, the more money you make. I maintain my own website. I use Photoshop but there's drag-and-drop programs like

FrontPage that are really simple to use. You don't really need much. As long as you have a presentable page it's up twenty-four hours. I got a hit counter that only I can see. To promote it I go to other sites and put blogs up. The more stuff you do, the better the likelihood that search engines will pull your name up when people are doing various searches on the web. People in their mind always think there's a huge cost associated with things when really that's not the case.

Q: Before we wrap up I want to return to the question I asked earlier about your influences. Who are some of the people you pattern yourself after artistically?

SO: I do my own thing. I don't pattern myself after anybody. I'm coming with my own thing. I'm coming with my own label. I'm coming with my own music. I want years from now for someone to say I'm doing what I'm doing because of Shake-O Blaize.

PR: Definitely I pattern my life after the Isley Brothers. As a band they went out and looked at popular artists and they were more interested in if you were good and not your race or even the genre you were in. If you were nasty they were going to cover your song and make it their own. That's one thing that I don't think enough artists do today. They do covers and they try to sound similar to the original whereas a lot of the songs that I dig were covers from other artists and the Isley brothers rocked 'em.

I would also add Bob Dylan to that list, too. I have more in common with Bob Dylan than I have with D'Angelo and Cee-lo. People are always comparing me to Gnarls Barkley. One of Bob's powers was that he wrote about the times and he didn't do it in the format that was accepted. I'm trying to be a vanguard too. When you want to be a shepherd the sheep aren't going to follow just because you say you're a shepherd. It's the same with being a preacher. You can say you're a preacher but how do you watch over your flock? How do you guide your flock? I hope that as my career expands my flock will understand that I'm not the type of singer that's interested in the trappings that come along with singing.

CR: I love to see urban people doing what they say we can't do. Sly and the Family Stone, Bad Brains, a lot of that shit opened my mind to a whole 'nother world of what you can do with music. Bad Brains changed my life. To see a black group doing hardcore punk in the eighties was powerful. I really, really respect them cats that take risks. You gotta appreciate that. You know they set the foundation for whatever we can do now. Cats that were like, "I can do this shit myself." Or who said, "I'm not going to go the traditional route." I'm black and I can do rock 'n roll and I don't have to be Jimi Hendrix. I have nothing against Jimi. I love him. But black people, white people, people in general, do not allow each other to have another view of doing rock 'n roll than Jimi Hendrix. It's like he's our savior and our devil. Black people didn't even give Hendrix respect when he was around, the same with Bob Marley. But then black people are the same people that complain about white people stealing our music or the same people that say something like, "you doing white boy shit." We set up so many reasons for why we fail but we cut each other's wings. We don't let each other fly. Yes! I'm from the hood and I listen to rock 'n roll!

VI.
MONEY. MONEY. MONEY.

From 1979-85, I lived in East Elmhurst, a neighborhood in Queens. The neighborhood's claim to fame is that it was the last place Malcolm X lived before he was assassinated. From '85 to '88, I lived in Manhattan. And then '88 to not that long ago I lived in Corona. Corona was a cool neighborhood to grow up in. It's like any "hood," black people, Hispanic people, working people, some poor people. It was never a run-down area. You go to Queens and see houses. There are more houses in East Elmhurst than in Corona, but there are still a lot of houses there too. That's one thing about Queens that's real deceptive. The houses give the impression that it's the suburbs. It's not. People are going through the same shit like in any hood. Some people just had houses.

Growing up, money was generally slim in my household. My father always worked. My mom worked off and on. Sometimes there was decent money. Sometimes there was no money. I've been in welfare hotels. I've been in shelters. But my parents always did the best they could. That I can say. We were just basically a poor, working class family from Corona. Because we didn't have any money I really didn't care about money. If I sold tapes with my father I had a little. When I was eight, nine years old I used to go to the Key Food on 99th St. and Astoria Blvd. to carry bags. I'd make ten dollars for a couple of hours work, which if you think about it is good money at that age. That's a lot of candy. But I didn't want to always hustle. A lot of times I just didn't want to work. So I didn't really have money.

The only person I knew who had money growing up was my Aunt Goodney. She's my father's sister. She's twenty years older than my father. My father was the youngest child. Aunt Goodney was a nurse in D.C., the head nurse at St. Elizabeth's Hospital in fact. She came up from Virginia and worked and worked and bought a house with her husband. And then she worked more. She worked a total of fifty years. She would always tell us that she had money because she worked. She wasn't rich. She had cars. She had fur coats. But no one gave her that shit. She earned it.

Every summer we'd go down to D.C. to see my aunt if we passed our grade and didn't have to do summer school. We'd leave in June and come back in late August, two full months out of New York. That was our reward. In my house we'd be scratching to eat then we'd go to D.C. and it was like a whole different story. The house was nice. The refrigerator was always full. We rode around in cars. My aunt wouldn't just give us anything we wanted because she was a hard working person, but it was nice. I enjoyed it. It was inspirational. It was a different world because it gave us a sense of stability.

Even though I had my aunt, no one actually *taught* me about money: how to manage it, how not to waste it, what a bank was for. My father was never good with money. My mother didn't teach me much about money either. Everything I've learned about money has been through experience, through trial and error. I'm by no means an expert on the subject. That being said, I do know how to manage the money I make and that alone separates me from a lot of independent artists I come in contact with. When it's a hundred degrees outside I don't *have* to come out. If I wake up and it's pouring down rain, I don't *have* to come out. I might not make any money that day but a day is not going to kill me. A week ain't going to kill me. If need be I can get out of the country today. God forbid if something like 9/11 happens again and I can't come out for two weeks because the city is on lock down, I'm not going to drown. I have built myself a life preserver. A lot of cats out here can't say that because they don't have a dime put away. It's not necessarily because I'm a better artist or even a better salesman. There are a lot of cats out here who hustle well. Some of them are pretty damn good. They just don't put money away. Every time they make a dime, they spend it. I've seen guys make five, six, even seven hundred dollars in a day, and be broke the next. They'll party the shit away and be asking to borrow money the next.

I've said it before and I'll say it again, there are going to be up days and down days so always prepare for the worst. You have to be ahead of the game. For example, when it's a bill week I'm not paying my bills with money I made that week. I'm paying my bills with money I made three weeks earlier. And when I don't have a bill week, I'm putting at least 80% of the money I make away. That's a rule I live by.

Out here it's your job to balance your own books. It's your *job*. Even though we're out on the street this is still the music business. This is a key point. This is a business and we're businesspeople. The only difference is that maybe we're not dealing with the fat cat sitting behind a desk who doesn't even care about hip-hop but who's getting rich off it. Out here we are our own managers and accountants. We make the product, sell the product and collect the profit.

We're responsible for all our expenses. We don't get a corporate expense account. There is no petty cash for daily expenditures. Living in a city like New York is expensive period. Just to ride to the city everyday. Just to eat! All of that adds up. Five dollars for lunch everyday is $25 every week, $100 a month, $1,200 a year. After a certain amount of time that all adds up. If you don't develop some kind of system to conduct your business properly you're not going to be able to do your music effectively. Your system doesn't have to be complex, just effective.

A lot of what's been said in this book so far has been about *making* money. We've talked about developing the right mindset, about dealing with customers, about being creative in your marketing and promotion strategies. But in reality it's not making the money that's difficult for most cats who hustle. If you come out here everyday you should never have a problem making money. While the days vary and the seasons vary, people are always buying records. I've sold to every type of person you can imagine. I've had some of my best days when it's raining outside. We live in a world of buyers and sellers. That's all there is, people who buy and people who sell. When you're outside everyday you start to see that. When you're sitting on the train you see kids selling candy. You see people playing music, break dancing, panhandling—those are all hustles. In America we're simply trained to think of work as something you do in an office. That's not the case, though. People are making money in all types of ways.

But like I said, it's not *making* the money that matters. It's *managing* it. Money management is one of the most difficult things in the world. We've talked about the promotional aspect of being an artistpreneur. Setting up a legal entity to protect yourself, getting your name out there, being present and available; being digital, following

80

through. Making sure the product is as good as it can be before you sell it. Now, it's time to talk about the managerial aspect. One of the hardest things for me to start doing was putting money in the bank. I still don't put *all* of my money in the bank now. When you are not raised to think of a bank as a place to house your money, it's an adjustment. You get used to living a certain way over time. You're essentially putting your trust in an institution. It's necessary, though. Banks are federally insured. Cash under the mattress isn't. Money in the bank, especially an investment bank like ING, makes money just by sitting there. Cash under the mattress loses value over time simply due to inflation. Money in the bank gives you leverage in case you need a loan or a line of credit in the future to help your business expand. Cash under the mattress doesn't exist in the banking world.

A businessperson can't afford to be afraid of the banking apparatus. You have to learn how to use it to your advantage. One way to do that is by setting up separate accounts, a business account and an account for you. That way you don't ever mess with your business money. For practical and legal reasons your business should always be separate. Practically speaking, if you know you're not good with money then having separate accounts is the safest way not to be broke. Keep in mind we run a cash operation. There's nothing better or worse than being paid in cash. It's great because it's there and it exists in a tangible form. It's terrible because it's so easy to spend it. Someone like Shake-O knows he can't keep cash on him, though. He's honest with himself. If it's green he's spending it. So any money he makes in a day he puts in the bank by the end of the day, or at the latest by the next morning. That takes **discipline.** He knows he will spend it otherwise so he removes the temptation. When you go to the bank to make a deposit, you can split your money up right then and there. Take out what you need in your pocket and put the rest of it in the business account. Just dump it in there and leave it. I recommend not even looking at the statements. Then, whenever you need something that has to do with your business operations, you'll always have it. Separate accounts assures that you'll have the money to keep **reinvesting** in yourself, which is something a lot of cats struggle with. Legally speaking, if something was to ever happen and your business is found liable, your personal funds will be protected. If, on the other hand, you're commingling funds, everything you have can be fair game for a creditor.

A businessperson always **sets strict spending limits** for themselves. Before they even go into a situation they know what they're willing to spend and they're not going over that amount *no matter what*. People always tend to overspend when they're out shopping. You're out. Everybody around you is spending money. You see something you like. It's on sale. You figure you deserve it. You figure it's not going to be there in a week or so. You go through this whole rationalization process so you splurge on yourself. When you're supporting yourself independently you really can't afford to do that. It's not like a regular job. You're not guaranteed a regular paycheck every week. Who doesn't like buying new sneakers and new clothes? But I'd rather buy that stuff after I've flipped my money and I know whatever I spend isn't going to a hurt me in a week or two. You have to set limits and stick to them.

One of the best pieces of advice anyone ever gave me about managing money was to always to ask myself: **What do I need**? Not what do I want. What do I need? If you ask yourself that question every time you're about to buy something, I guarantee you'll see a change in your spending habits. I might *want* a new pair of sneakers but buying them might set my business plans back a week. I might need $1,300 to put out my record and I only have $800 in the bank. I could go out for a week and make $100 a day, cut off $15 for expenses, and have the money in a week. But if I go buy a pair of $85 sneakers, then I've not only lost a day's work I've set my album back a week. A week might not sound like a long time, but in the world of the independent businessperson it is. A week is not only time, it's quality. If you get set back a week, then chances are you're going to try to make that time back up by cutting some other corner. Ultimately, something along the way will come up short. In my opinion the most dangerous creation of the last fifteen years is the **ATM** card. I just got one myself two years ago and I still don't carry it with me. I'm old enough to remember there not being ATM cards, but most kids coming up today have been raised with them. They live their lives with ATM cards. They don't carry cash, but it's the same thing because you have complete access to your money at all times. There's a money machine on every corner, in every bodega. Society makes that seem like a good thing. It's *good* to be able to get money whenever you need it, wherever you need it, however much you need. It's *good* to be able to buy whatever you want when you want it. They make it seem like cards are *better* than cash. Well, I disagree. Not because I'm a conspiracy theorist who's worried about having my transactions monitored and tracked. Not because I'm worried about some secret agency collecting and distributing information they've gathered about me. I disagree because you don't see the money go. It's an illusion. Cards trick you into thinking you've got an endless supply of money. Maybe some people would rather not see their money dwindle little by little. Not me. I like to see my money leave my hand. I like to feel it in my pocket. I need to constantly be reminded that I don't have enough. As long as Bill Gates is alive I'll never have enough.

I've seen kids that come out with a week's worth of cash so they can front like they're making money. They think it's cute. They'll bring a thousand dollars out like they made it one day. That's stupid. Not only are you're tempting yourself, you're lying to yourself. The really shrewd cat doesn't even come out of the house with any money. Shake-O will come out with a Metro card and a bag of CDs. That's it. If he doesn't sell his CDs then he doesn't have anything. If he doesn't make money then he doesn't eat. That's putting your back against the wall everyday. You have to face that fear of being broke daily. You're reminded of where you been before and how much you don't want to be back in that place. Personally, I bring $5 for lunch. But I don't eat before I make a sale. It could be two o'clock but if I haven't made a sale I'm not taking a lunch break. And if I don't make money all day, then I'm not going home until I do. That's a rule I live by. Why go home if you haven't earned any money? It doesn't make sense. It sounds drastic, but you have to train yourself. We live in a consumer society where the temptation to spend, spend, spend is all around you. In order to survive out here, your spending should be attached to your work. You should deserve that meal. You ain't doing nothing just you 'cause you come out. You gotta earn that lunch.

My first year coming out I noticed something that's stuck with me. There might've been three people outside, but the whole block would be lined up with vendors. These were people who weren't from America and they were up and ready. That left a huge impression on me because it showed me exactly what it means to be independent. You can see why people from outside the country say Americans are spoiled. It's not that we don't want to work. We just aren't taught how to hustle. We're scared of getting dirty. You can't look pretty all the time. My feeling is get dirty then get pretty. It feels good to get pretty after you've been dirty. A hard day's hustle is a beautiful thing. There's nothing like taking a shower after you've been beating the pavement all day. *I honestly believe that the everyday hustle should be in everybody's life.* It keeps you hungry and focused on making money and not on shit that's not important. In anything you do, if you're going to be a doctor or a lawyer—anything, you have to hustle. You have to do it every single day. The more you come out, the more people you know, the better off you are in your career. Even when I take a day off to relax and unwind that just means I'm writing, making music, trying to get studio sessions going. Even if you don't see me on the block with a CD in hand, you better believe I'm somewhere preparing for another CD. I'm an acrobat with this. And if it don't flip then that means I need a new package. Like I said before, I'm still poor. I'm just not broke like I was before. I *refuse* to be broke.

VII.
STRENGTH OF TEAM

I f I had to choose my ideal football team the 1995 Dallas Cowboys would be at the top of my list. Why? They were a great team. They had great offensive talent: Troy Aikman, Emmit Smith, Jay Novacek; Michael Irvin, a sick defense, Ken Norton, Deon Sanders, Charles Haley, Nate Newton. Everyone was popping. Everyone was dominant at their position. The whole team operated in unison. They were a machine. And they believed they could win every game. My ideal basketball team would have to be the Bulls team that went seventy-two and ten. They had Michael Jordan, Scottie Pippen, Dennis Rodman, Toni Kukoc and a bunch of other players. Just thinking about that shit brings tears to my eyes. Everyone knew their roles. Everyone was playing at their best. The team was so much better than the individuals that some guys were playing past their abilities. Rodman was always good but he wasn't doing what he was doing then his entire career. He was going and grabbing twenty-two rebounds some nights. He averaged fifteen a game. The man literally retarded his offense because the team didn't need that from him. You had Jordan who could do whatever he wanted on the court. What they needed was for him to rebound and shut down the other team's top scorer. He would make players a non-factor in the game.

Those were teams right there.

Those teams also remind you that sometimes it's not all about talent. Too many great players can sometimes cancel each other. Look at USA Basketball teams the last few years. They have more talent than any other team in the world and yet the best they've done in the past two major international competitions is third place. I have people I grew up with that I honestly would put up against anybody because they're just as talented or more talented, lyrically. But is it active talent? Are they doing something to make the world aware of their talent? No. But I honestly know in my heart of hearts that these guys are way better than other cats. Not just better; way better. But if they don't have the will power to make it happen—to get their voice out there and be heard—then it doesn't matter. Talent without discipline and work ethic means nothing.

I learned that lesson from my first group, Triflicts. We didn't work hard enough to be successful. Obviously the times were a little different. I was a teenager, early twenties. We were kids. We were just trying to get nice. We'd write the same song six times. We didn't understand work ethic. We were just really good. I thought I didn't have to be out here hustling because I had too much talent. I thought the only people that are out in the street are people who can't get signed. People are so surprised when they hear my shit. They'll be like, "Dude, you're really talented. You're the truth." The street has a negative connotation. Street equals bootleg in people's minds.

That whole experience with Triflicts taught me humility. When I stopped rhyming with them I knew I had to step the shit up. Being in a group, you have more time and more opportunity to gain listeners. If a listener doesn't like me they still might like someone else in the group so they'll still buy the record. As a solo artist that can't happen. I had to realize that. You have to catch people's attention quicker. Then, as far as style, I incorporated some of their shit into my shit and put it all together to create something. You have to be that group as one person.

My second group taught me that too much talent and not enough execution equals a whole lotta wasted potential. I learned that just saying you're a leader doesn't make you a leader. You have to lead by example. You have to do a lot of maintenance. I learned a lot from that experience. We gotta lot of songs. I thought with a collective you can pop more. Five, six people, means you can get everybody. You can't make people want shit, though. A lot of cats are scared to put themselves out there. I remember we went to Rock Steady once four years ago with our mix tape. We had a bag full of them. And these cats were watching the show. I couldn't believe it. We were there because we were supposed to be making money and spreading our music. They didn't want to do anything to make the team stronger. They were happy to have it all on my shoulders, then when things fell through they could put the blame on me. That experience turned me off to the idea of being in a group again. In fact, since that experience I've become more or less my own one-man gang. I can't afford to wait for other people anymore. Even the people in my circle are their own people. They're not on my team. If you can get a team together, though, you can take it to that next level.

Ideally to be really successful as an artistpreneur you get three to five people who are on the same page that want to make money. I want people around me who are like, "I believe in the shit you do and I want to make money." I'm on some fifty-fifty shit. I'd rather sell 20,000 CDs and get that $5 from my partner than try to do it all on my own. I go out of town now and there's nobody making money on this strip. But if I go out of town and I got a team then they're making money and I'm making money. I'm in Jersey making money and they're in New York. That's a deal. But it's hard to find people who are willing to treat your product like it's theirs. You gotta make it worth their time. People have to be comfortable and involved. My advice to younger cats coming up is that you really have to make sure everyone around you is doing something. If the dude is just getting your covers make sure he's getting them on time. If you're going out of town make sure that other dude is there making money. Or, little by little start weeding people out. If there are five of you and only two of you are doing the work then you two need to go hard together and leave the others behind. You might think you'll get less done but if the two of you are really running hard you can really make things happen.

Sometimes it's hard when someone close to you is holding you back. But just like you check yourself you gotta check them too. You have to take inventory. Is this person beneficial to my life? It's not personal. It's a simple question. Are they moving my life forward? This is not an easy thing to do. But you put your life on pause for this shit. This is your business. You can't just give time and money away to people who aren't carrying their weight. You have to cut your losses. It is your life. I realized this like five years ago when dudes I grew up with were making like $70,000 a year. Some of the same dudes I went to GED school with. Not high school, GED school. They'll tell you Creature is smarter than me. I realized I didn't want to get rich doing what somebody else wanted me to do. I wanted to get rich doing what I want to do. If your heart is not into something you're not going to put that extra effort into it. That's the shit that wakes you up and gets you out of bed.

You put your life on pause for your dreams to get accomplished and you have to always remember that. It's different, just not even havin' children. All your friends are having families and you gotta hold it down. I can't be having children yet. A lot of my people not doing music have kids. All my music people just started having kids two years ago. They're just now doing that. These cats are in their thirties. They had to put that family shit on pause until they were ready. You have to sacrifice for what you want. You have to. I ran into my dude recently. This cat was nasty on the mike. He's incredible. But I told him how much I respected his decision to stop doing music. He's got two sons and a wife and music ain't paying the bills. It's that simple. He can't gamble on it enough right now. If I was in the situation, you have to make that decision. When I think about my people from Insomniac, they ain't have no excuses. They didn't have kids. They didn't have wives. You gotta put the pedal to the metal and make that shit happen.

If you ask me the RZA is a genius in this regard. He's got to be one of the smartest people in the world. How can you pull what he pulled with the Wu off? They didn't all like each other. But they stood together for a common goal. They stuck to their original plan. They didn't let a bunch of outsiders on their albums. Until they got their own names out there they weren't letting hardly anybody rhyme on their records. The Wu fed a lot of people. The original nine plus Cappadonna plus all the other groups like Sons of Man, Killa Bees; Killa Army. Then you got cats that got solo careers from there. Wu fed a lot of muthafuckas. And they changed the game. They signed a group deal without signing everyone to individual deals. That way they went out and got solo deals from other labels. I don't know how RZA paid people but it got done. I look up to that guy a lot. To manage egos but at the same time to cater to them is some shit. He had to be father, mother, psychiatrist, boss, comrade—RZA! That kid is crazy! He rhymes too but he decided to fall back because he understood what was going to work. Women were going to feel Method Man more. Ol Dirty Bastard had a popular appeal. It takes vision and humility. He understood the importance of having his artists on all different labels. It kept things from getting too competitive on the inside and gave them a presence on other labels. Not only that, the level of talent in the Wu is unparalleled. Ninety percent of that click is top notch MCs. They're on point. You don't get that from clicks no more. From Wu a lot of people started seeing the strength in numbers.

If you can't have a team in that sense then the next best thing is to link with what I call Comrades in Arms. These are other people with a general's mentality, people who are leaders themselves. I work with Shake-O for example. I'm comfortable hustling with him because we don't ask anything from each other. Our mentality is the same: go hard. It's an unspoken thing between us. He calls me; I call him. We get each other out. He's not going to hit me up for $100. I'll give it to him if he really needs it, but he's his own man and he's responsible for himself. We're both hustlers. We both love the game. I love to come out with no money and look at my pocket at the end of the day and see a bunch of dough I made that day. He's the same way.

Generally, someone who is consistent and positive, that's who I work alongside out here, someone who has a generally positive outlook on life and a strong work ethic. Percee P. is a great example of this. He's signed to Stone's Throw and he's still out here hustling. I've seen him get off stage and go talk to people. He makes it real for people. You can touch him. He's tangible. That's the kind of person I want to be around. Not someone who jumps out whenever there's a camera and runs their spiel and you don't see them again for months.

By the same token, if a person's mentality is negative, if they're always complaining about what they don't have and what others have, then I can't be bothered. I can't keep pushing this train when you brought too much luggage. Pack light. Bring a book bag and maybe a duffel bag. Don't bring your whole life with you. C'mon man. I have to cut people off, can't deal with people that's too much headache. It's a waste. I gotta constantly check people. I'm not here for certain things.

Helpful Reminders

- ☐ **Associations**: If you can't rely on a strong team for support you should build associations with people. Associations are not necessarily friendships. They're acquaintanceships. These are people who can vouch for you, who connect you with opportunities and such. I make it a point to know someone on every important independent label out here. That's social capital.
- ☐ **Real Recognizes Real**: At the end of the day people respect the hustle. If you don't have a team, you can always find comrades who have a similar vision.
- ☐ **Beat the Pavement**: Why do you deserve to be heard? You only deserve to be heard when you make people hear you. You only make people hear you when you outwork them. There's always some kid somewhere writing a hundred raps a day who's hungry. You gotta be that kid.
- ☐ **Beware those Back-stabbers**: Everyone is not going to be happy for your success. Everybody you're around is not going to be supportive of you. Listen to the language. Everybody doesn't want you

to do well. You don't need to be around people who aren't supporting you.

☐ **Spread Wisdom**: I've been helped by a lot of people; we all have to support one another's dreams and give one another guidance. That's teamwork in action.

☐ **The Come-Up**: There's a reason why a lot of people give up on their dreams. It's hard and it gets lonely. People just want to look at the exterior image. Relish the grind. Love the hustle.

VIII.
A STAR IN
YOUR OWN MIND

I've talked a lot about producing and selling your music independently. Obviously these are crucial elements to surviving as an artist. But what you can't overlook or undervalue is the performance side of your artistry. You have to keep in mind that a lot of people don't see hip-hop artists as skilled professionals. That's because a lot of mediocre acts have been commercially successful and because the live performances at too many hip-hop shows are sub-par. As artists we have to protect the integrity of the art form. By that I mean this. Hip-hop was born in the streets. It was cultivated on corners. The torchbearers were showmen whose reputations depended upon their live performances. Before, making an album meant something. You had a voice. You'd proven yourself on stage. These days the standards have been lowered. In fact, too often it's the very opposite. Cats put out records before they've paid their dues. Sometimes they've never even performed in front of a live audience. It's cool that everybody has access to technology. What's not cool, though, is that just because you have that access you think you're a recording artist. It's deeper than that. You really have to put in the work. It's not just about recording an album, pressing it up and selling it to people as "real hip-hop". I performed for almost three years before I even recorded a demo. I was in the street. I was on the corner. I was doing shows. I had already performed thirty, forty times before I ever even went into a booth. Now kids have two albums and have never done a single show, not one. They don't know what to do when they step on stage. This chapter is about one thing and only one thing: **performing**.

1. <u>Study the Great Ones</u>

Knowing your craft isn't just knowing how to do it; it's knowing how it's been done in the past. The great ones in any arena are students of their craft. That's what separates them from everyone else. This is different than listening to an album and memorizing the lyrics and learning the flow. In order to be a good performer you have to study what good performers do. How do they engage their audience? What kind of energy do they offer? There are even some people who don't have all the skills but who have stage presence. They don't need fifteen people surrounding them to make them look good. They have certain intangible qualities that make their performance stand on its own. HR from Bad Brains, KRS-One, Busta Rhymes, this underground cat named Brother Ali, Method Man and Redman, the Roots, these people are showmen. You can't leave these people's shows and not be like, "Damn!" You don't even necessarily have to like their music all that much. KRS-One is a dominant force on

96

stage. Why is that? It's diction. It's energy; it's crowd control.

Something I do is buy old performances on video or DVD. I've watched Ritchie Haven's performance at Woodstock several times. Now, if anybody really knows the story, they only gave him like ten minutes but he was up there for three hours because all the other acts couldn't get there. So he just sat up there and played and played and played in front of hundreds of thousands of people. After three hours you can tell he's huffing for real. His eyes were blood shot. But he was so focused. He's out there keeping beat with his leg and he's worn a groove in his guitar and his dashiki is stuck to his back. And when he gets to the final note he's spinning around and playing and singing. The band is playing and it's amazing, absolutely amazing. That's what the audience comes to see, though. They want to be wowed. They want you to take them some place they've never been. And that requires you as the artist offering everything you have. Look at it this way. If you don't have a left on the court but you still have a strong right you're always going to be okay but you'll never make it in the NBA. Being on stage is like taking a step toward the NBA.

2. Practice Makes Perfect

You can't just get on stage and put on a track. It's just not that simple. You have to rehearse like any other performer. Whether it's in front of the mirror or in a studio, it's imperative; it's not simply about getting on stage and telling people how dope you are. I once was at this competition with this kid who was talking all this shit. "Yeah, yeah I'm thorough. I'ma do

97

it. I'ma shut it down." He spent two minutes talking about how nice he was and then he turned around and forgot his lines. He couldn't get through one line. I can't tell you how many shows I've sat through over the last fifteen years where people have gotten on stage and have no business being up there. They weren't prepared. They didn't know how to hold a mike, how to connect with the crowd. Rehearsal is the only way you figure out what you do well and don't do well. If you don't rehearse you forget your own songs. Rehearsal time is important because you get to work your kinks out. Mistakes you make in practice will be the mistakes you make live. Rehearsal also gives you the opportunity to prepare for the worst case scenario. What if there's a problem with the mike? How are you going to handle that? Sometimes I rehearse sick versions of songs in case I have a chest cold. I try to rehearse songs in different keys so that if I have to adjust my voice it still sounds good. That way it becomes second nature to me.

3. <u>Competitions/ Open Mikes/Compilation Albums</u>

Once you've studied some and practiced a lot you're ready to try performing. The question is where. Open mikes and competitions are always a good option. But there's a few things you should take into consideration before you go in that direction. Most competitions and open mike contests are rigged. If the competition is based on crowd participation where the crowd chooses the winner and you come with a hundred people, then chances are you're going to win. I once did a contest where I had to sell tickets in order to compete. The deal was the organizers get like forty artists to sign-up and compete in a single night. The top performers were supposed to move on to the next round until there was a champion. Well, before I even got on they started handing out flyers for the next round and it's got the five winners who will be competing for the title. And I hadn't even performed yet! So I went up to the judge and let them know that I knew what was up. That's how they make money in the music industry, though. Another way is through those compilation albums where you give the producer a certain amount of money to put you on. This one woman tried to tell me that if I paid her one thousand dollars she'd put me on an album that was going to be heard by forty-thousand people. No way!

As a rule, if I have to pay you to perform in your competition then there's a problem. Think about it. They're providing a venue and offering a competition. What is it they need, a registration fee? They're charging people to come in, right? So why do they need money from the performers? See, people get caught up, though. They think there are going to be A&Rs there and they risk it. My advice is to follow your instincts. If you have to pay for an open mike it probably ain't worth it. You should maybe pay an entrance fee, but that's it. Anything else—drink minimums, mandatory ticket sale quotas—is a bunch of B.S.

If you do choose to go to open mikes understand this: they're cliquish. You have to make sure you shake the hand of the cat that runs the open mike after you get off stage because if they don't know you you're in trouble. I've gone places and signed up to perform and waited three or four hours to finally get on stage after they've allowed all their friends who signed up after me to perform. But, if you make sure you introduce yourself to the people who run the event that makes a world of difference. You might start as the underdog but if you put in that work and you have talent they have to eventually recognize you.

Keep this in mind, though. I once read about James Brown's first performance at the Apollo. He threw his towel into the crowd and they threw it back at him. They threw James Brown's towel back in his face! Someone once told me that the great ones never win competitions and I believe that's true. A lot of singers we really idolize lost all their talent competitions. They never got the grand prize. What does that tell you?

4. <u>Booking Shows</u>

No matter what people say there are an abundance of shows, especially in cities like New York. The question is whether the show is paying or not. There might not be any money involved at all. That shit is a little tricky because a lot of it is relationships. I often gets shows from others shows, which is again why it's so important to prepare. People generally aren't going to come, beating down your door. You have to be at your best at all times and be seen as frequently as possible, but you also can't exploit yourself by doing everything for nothing. I might take a short doing a show but sometimes it's worth it. If you're opening for someone that everyone is talking about and you get enough time to be heard then people are going to be talking about you too. It gives you more credibility even though it might not pay. But like I said before, you can't be afraid of getting paid. Know your value and put your value on the table otherwise people are going to take advantage of you. There really is no tried and true method for booking shows as an independent artist. If you have a manager and a publicist it can be a lot easier, of course, but even then that all depends on whether you've proven yourself as a bankable commodity.

5. The Day of a Show

I believe visualization is the first step to reality. So the day of a show I typically try to treat myself like the star that I am. Different people have different ways of preparing. If I don't have to come out of the house that day then I don't. I might go over a set. I might practice a whole show just so I can keep shit fresh in my head. I'll just kind of bum around. Listen to music that inspires me. Lift some weights. Shower. Whatever it takes to stay loose and in that focused zone. I'm working my spirit into the right place and I'm trying not to have any distractions that can take any of that energy away. Preacher calls it "Rock Star Thursdays" even though it's more about whatever day the show is on. The idea is that for that day he treats himself like a megastar. He'll get the food he wants. He'll drink the beverages he wants. He'll play video games. He'll smoke his performance weed. Whatever he needs to feel like a super-champion, that's what Rock Star Thursdays are all about.

Once I get to the venue I typically turn my phone off. I've had too many people call me asking to get them on the list when I'm trying to get ready to go on stage. I don't want to be bothered with that. I shouldn't have to be bothered with that. As an artist you have to be selfish. It's easy when you have a bunch of handlers around catering to you, but you still have to do it even when you're the underdog. You have to see yourself in a certain light.

Some people can get fucked up and still remember everything. I know I can't do that. I have to focus on the shit I'm saying. Some people can smoke five blunts before a performance and not miss a beat on stage. Every word will be perfect. They'll hear that bell and they'll be on. Really it's about knowing yourself. Knowing what brings out the best in you. Preacher likes to catch a buzz before he goes on stage. It chills him out because he has a lot of nervous energy. It does the exact opposite for me. I only get nervous energy when I have to wait too long. If you tell me I'm supposed to go on at a certain time then I want to go on at that time. If I have to wait then I get irritable. It's like warming up to play a game and then finding out it's delayed. You're ready to jump on the court. It throws you off.

But see here's where the professionalism comes through. I've felt like leaving a lot. I channel that frustration into my performance. I get extra focused. The promoters did that with a Papoose show we did in Brooklyn. They kept pushing us and pushing us and when we got on stage two and a half, three hours after we were supposed to, we destroyed it. I let people know that I was pissed. I was trying to run people off the stage, straight up. The key is not to get discouraged by the setbacks. It's the nature of this business but you have to persevere.

6. <u>The Performance</u>

The stage is where you have the opportunity to set things straight. You might not have the marketing budget behind you but that doesn't matter when the show starts. Live shows are my thing. They are the real reason why I stopped drinking and smoking. When I was performing as a kid I didn't drink or smoke but I'd be high from my performance. When you kill a show and you know you left it all on the stage there's nothing like it. You can't pay for that. When I'm on stage I'm high off the adrenaline; euphoria overcomes me. The stage is where everything that has happened throughout the day is now being dropped at my feet. That's the energy. That's the part of the performance that's about me, the artist. The other part is about the audience.

An artist's relationship with the audience depends on their personality. It depends on what facets they bring out when they're on stage. But an artist also has to be aware of that persona and have developed it into a weapon. If you're trying to create a hyped atmosphere then you have to project that. If you're trying to create a sensual atmosphere then you have to project that. If you don't have a clue about what your image is then you're going to project that too. The more time you spend on stage, the more comfortable you are and the more you begin to read people's non-verbal reactions. Once you come out of your own shell, which is typically the case for a lot of young artists, you can focus in on people and draw them in. You can see who's moving; who's not moving. If someone is talking during my show I don't ignore them, I rhyme at them. If I can get close to them then I'm going to literally rhyme in their face. Every time someone talks during my set I let it be known that I'm not happy about it. It's insulting. I've done shows on the road where people have made it clear that they're not there to see me perform. I'm still going to perform like you're the one playing yourself by not listening to me, though. I perform even harder. All I ask is for people's time during my set. That's all.

7. <u>Helpful Performance Tips</u>

- ☐ **Keep Working after the Show**: Sell CDs and talk to people who can further your career. A lot of people think they've earned extra Rock Star time. They want to hang out backstage. Get a drink. Kick it with people. Those are bad ideas. You have a golden opportunity to make money and network so use that time wisely. Be approachable and approach others.

- ☐ **Come with Something Special**: Preacher gives away chocolate at the door before all his shows. It's a nice thing for the ladies. It gets them in the mood. Maybe you give away a flyer or t-shirts. Just make it be something and make it be memorable.

- ☐ **Respect other Artists**: I've seen plenty of horrible performances and I've been tempted to heckle and laugh, but I don't. Regardless of a person's ability, you have to give them respect just for being up on the stage.

- ☐ **Don't Talk Shit Unless You are the Shit**: And if you are the shit then you don't have to talk shit. When you are conceited you only set yourself up for a downfall. You never know what's going to happen on stage. You could forget your lines. The speakers could blow out. One thing is for sure, though. If you come off arrogant people will seize the opportunity to kick you when you're down. Humility is essential.

☐ **Carry the Mantle with Pride**: Anything you do, you gotta do it seriously. Prepare, know your work, practice, study the greats and get out there and do it right.

Interlude #4: Duo Live

Profile

Quotable: "We haven't invented the wheel. We might've just put some rims on the shit but it was done way before us and it'll be done way after us."

Intelligence: Founding members Sid V. (right) and Fre (left) are street hustle pioneers. Started **Redemption Music Group** in 1996; toured with KRS-One, Lil Wayne, Young Jeezy and Dem Franchise Boys; sod more than 160,000 records on the street. Founded **Redemption Music Group** in 1996, a decade on the street, made more than 1.5 million dollars from hand-to-hand sales, signed independent distribution deal with Warner Brothers. First national released album to hit stores 02.06.07.

Stomping Grounds: NYC and Miami
Discography:
Niggalympics (1996)
DD7 (1997)
Duo Die (1999)
Mharch Madness (2000)
Faith feat, Angie Stone (2001)
We Invented the Freestyle Mix tape (2001)
Midnight Oil Mix CD (2002)
First H.I.Mpressions (2003)
Free Lunch: The Hood Gotta Eat (2004)
The Official Free Lunch Mix CD: Vol. 1 (2004)
The Official Free Lunch Mix CD: Vol. 2 (2005)
The Color of Money (2005)
That's What's Next (2006)
Website: www.redemptionmusicgroup.com

Growth and Transformation in the Street Hustle

Sid: We've been making music since '89 but we first had the idea of selling our music independently in '95. The process of getting the song together and putting it out took about a year. Ninety-Six we had our first release. We did vinyl first but it was really messed up because they put it on 45-speed. We decided to sell it anyway, friends, family. People we knew, walking down Fulton. Then we realized that people weren't buying vinyl like that. They were buying tapes. That's when we decided to press up tapes, one song on side A and an instrumental on side B. It was called *The Little Red Tape*.

Fre: At this time the only cats out there on the east coast were Uptown, Showbiz and AG, Wu-Tang. These cats were popping the trunk with vinyl. But no one had even transitioned into cassette at that time; not that we know of. We'd never seen no one actually hand-to-handing their cassette. We were kind of nervous about doing it because it was N.Y. and it was still a little wild on the street back then. It was coming off the cusp of the drug era. We were from the hood so we was trying to do it in the hood. We were a little bit leery because we didn't know how people was gonna take us runnin' up on them. You know. It was a little unnerving, but we noticed we was getting mad love. People appreciated it. From there we started going out to Green Acres Mall. We'd be in the parking lot all day selling it for five bucks.

From there we pioneered the Stop Light Hustle. We stood on the corner and waited for the light to turn red. Then we'd run up on as many cars as we could in the red light time, which is forty seconds. We had just enough time to say, "Listen, this is my stuff, I did it independent; check it out." And they're like, "I need to hear it." They pop it in and hear two seconds and literally you get the sale or you don't.

We had been offered a bunch of situations by major labels right around that time. Electra wanted to give us a situation. So did Atlantic. But they wanted us to water down our stuff and commercialize—basically conform—and the whole drive for us to do it wasn't initially to make money. It was to get our music out in a pure form. We all had jobs that were keepin' us sustained so we were doing it just for the love of the music. It developed over the years into a business. It really didn't even develop until 2003. We did it for seven years off love, every summer. Just for sport almost. Every summer we'd drop a new release. It developed into a business because every year—and this is something that a lot of these artists today who are doing it need to know—we improved the quality of the product. The only reason Duo Live and Redemption Recordings survived are two things. One is our team. We built a team that was strong and consistent and stuck together. That's one. And number two, the quality of the music always got better. Ninety-Six we had vinyl and cassette tapes. After that we had maxi-singles. Then we had a single cassette with a CD. We were the first cats to come the streets with CDs. *We* did that. That was the maxi-single, *Duo Die*. From 1996-2000 we were Duo Die. 1999 we brought out the CD with four joints on it and started selling it for $5.

Sid: The first single, like I said we got it professionally mixed and recorded. The vinyl came out fucked up. Our second single we got professionally mixed again at Hitmakers. We weren't even up to the level of mastering yet. A lot of people don't even understand that. Mastering is a level beyond mixing. A lot of these artists are putting out their records without getting them mastered. That's the icing on the cake. The first CD we did it in our crib. We recorded, mixed, and mastered it in the crib on some digital eight track shit. The songs were hot but the sound quality was shitty. We were working with what we had, though. After that we put out our first album, *Mharch Madness*. That was 2000.

Fre: That was the first time, after four years of grinding for first $3 then $5, that we sold our stuff for $10. Once again, *this is a process*. It wasn't until 2000 that we came with a full CD. It was fully packaged, shrink-wrapped. It had a full-color booklet inside. That was $10. I buy everything on the street but I tell cats who have a CD that they printed at home on a CD-R that they wrote on without a cover or a cover they printed at home, that they're selling for $10 that it's not $10. And that's no disrespect. That's just a lesson for you to understand that you need to step up your game because there are people out there with fully packaged products they're selling for $10 and that takes away from their hustle. It's like the drug game. You come out selling gigantic bags of bush weed and everybody else is selling quality reefer you're fucking the game up for the rest of the brothers and we supposed to be working together.

Sid: So we recorded that first album in a major studio. It was a blessing because Fre's cousin Jimmy Cozier was signed to J Records so we recorded a lot of the album during the down time of his sessions. We threw that out there. That was good. We sold about 6,000 copies of that just in the summer. That was when we first really made some money. We had never made any substantial money to write home about before that. We made like $50,000 in a summer. We started to get into the marketing aspect, which was also ahead of its time on the street level. We had t-shirts. We had postcards.

Fre: We started developing the team at that time too,

three or four heads, friends and family. It was like in a way sending your kids somewhere so they could stay out of trouble. We was in the 'hood so to a certain extent it was good for us and for the cats who came with us, because we wouldn't have been doing nothing but being on the block getting caught up. It was a way to get away from the drama. Then we'd have some money to spend at night. You know. That's another thing that people lose sight of when they see cats out there doing their thing independently. It saved us from the perils of the streets. It was something constructive and recreational to keep us out of the ghetto. That's a reason we started employing people. "Yo, he's going to get in trouble. Let's get him down." That's how we developed into a team. All of a sudden we were wearing the same t-shirts.

Sid: That was 2000. 2001 Fre links up with Angie Stone and she eventually finds out that Fre did music. She loved our music so basically this alliance was formed between us and Angie that led to us collaborating on a song for our label. This was our first time doing something with a major artist and the first time collaborating with anyone outside of our family. We put this song out called "Faith" featuring her, strictly vinyl. That was big for us. That got bootlegged in Japan. It made its way to South Africa. Wendy Williams played it in daytime rotation. This was the first time a major radio station ever played us.

Fre: Then we did a mix CD that same year. We were among the first clique of dudes to do their own mix CD. This was when 50 Cent came out with his. Artists weren't really doing that. We dropped *We Invented the Freestyle*.

Sid: That was a turning point for us because Fre killed the mix CD. People started to take us a little more seriously. It went from these guys sell their CDs in the street to their stuff is hot and they're dope. We started

111

developing a following after that. All of a sudden people wanted to have the Duo Live collection.

Fre: From 2000 to now we went crazy. We just put in work. In 2000 we dropped our first album. In 2001 we dropped the single with Angie. Then we dropped two mix tapes. 2002 we worked on our studio album and in 2003 we put out *First H.I.Mpressions*. That was the project that really took us to the next level. We sold nearly 30,000 records. This was when dudes decided to quit our day jobs and put our back against the wall. We got three of our partners, we bought the van, and we decided to get out of NY. We started in NYC. Sold like 6,000 here. Then we decided to go to Atlanta. We went there for a few weeks. Hit up Five Points, Little Five Points: same format, taking it all over the place. What we found was that Atlanta was a real working city so nothing really popped until the weekend. The hustle was decent but it wasn't what we were used to so we took a trip to Miami just to check the scene. When we saw South Beach....

Sid: We started hustling just that one day. It was popping. We decided to go back to Atlanta to get our stuff and came back with a thousand CDs and no money. We were broke. We had enough to get us to Miami. We got there, five of us. We slept in the truck for four days. We washed up on the beach. We lived like beach bums. We had nowhere to go. Four days later we had enough to get back to NYC so we could open for Jehru at SOB's.

Fre: When we got back to Miami we had enough money from those four days of hustling to get a hotel room in an extended stay hotel. Six of us lived in a hotel room for two months, all six of us. All we did was hustle seven days a week. We made enough to buy a duplex. A year later we bought a three-thousand square foot mansion and we got an office on Lincoln Road. When the operation was at its peak we had about twelve people on staff, two people doing reception, eight cats grinding, Fre and myself. We were making about $10,000 a week.

Sid: Being that Miami is a tourist attraction, everyone from the coldest parts of the country comes there. They'll buy CDs and take them back with them. In Miami a lot of people were buying and taking it back to places here in the US, people from the Midwest, South, West. Wherever. From then on we just never stopped. We put out two mix CDs that accompanied *Free Lunch*. That was another 30,000 CDs. Then we put out *The Color of Money* which has now sold more than 30,000 CDs.

Fre: All totaled we've sold about a 160,000 CDs. Of that you can honestly say that 140,000 have been sold at $10 a pop. We've made about a million and a half dollars. To this day—even though me and Sid are no longer in the streets—we've moved into a different zone, we're still 100 percent independent. We have an independent deal with Warner Brothers now. We're putting out a new version of *The Color of Money* for national distribution. It's still a grind for us. Now it's different is all, we're still doing the work. Now it's just way more work. Most days I wish I was in the street selling CDs because it's so much easier. All you have to do is sell your material and make money. Now we have to create a functioning label, govern sales beyond that which I can see and touch. We still use guerilla-marketing tactics but we also need traditional marketing as well. It's a lot more work and stress. This is also why I tell cats in the street to keep working on their art, keep perfecting their craft, because one day you come to a point when your music is going to have sell itself. If you're not prepared then you'll always be stuck in that place. If you feel like you're someone with a message to share with a wider audience then you have to prepare to get off the streets one day. And that's going to be with your art.

Our success proves that the underdog can always win and the underdog does win. It requires a manifesto. It requires rules to the game. It requires that we respect each other. Back in the days the soul cats was coming up off the Chitlin' Circuit. That's kind of what we're coming up off too. We're the farm team. But the farm team got championships. The farm team gets money. The farm team got fans.

Sid: My pops told me back in the day back in the sixties and early seventies Ritchie Havens used to be on the same streets.

Fre: Bob Marley used to do the same shit. Actually, in Trenchtown way before he ever bust, when he was still doing Ska, before the Wailers. He was hand-to-handing his music, going to different DJs trying to get them to play it. We haven't invented the wheel. We might've just put some rims on the shit but it was done way before us and it'll be done way after us. And I expect them to take it to the next level. We're just thankful to be a part of this, to be pioneers of this. At the end of the day this is independent black business.

IX.
HUSTLER'S
HALL OF FAME:

LEGENDARY
INDEPENDENT ARTISTS

Name: Too $hort

Government Name: Todd Anthony Shaw

Label: Founded **Dangerous Music** which became **$hort Records** and is now **Up All Night Music**

Stomping grounds: Oakland, CA and Atlanta, GA

Intelligence: Perhaps the most influential independent hustler of them all. $hort originally sold his tapes out of paper bags on the bus with his partner Freddie B. He perfected the art of the "Pause Mix," a 30-minute song with no hook using a simple cassette player. He had his first breakthrough song, *Freaky Tales*, on his independently released *Born to Mack* album in 1987. $hort went on to sell 50,000 copies of the album before it was re-released a year later by **Jive Records** following the double platinum success of *Life Is...Too $hort*. $hort has released 16 albums to date.

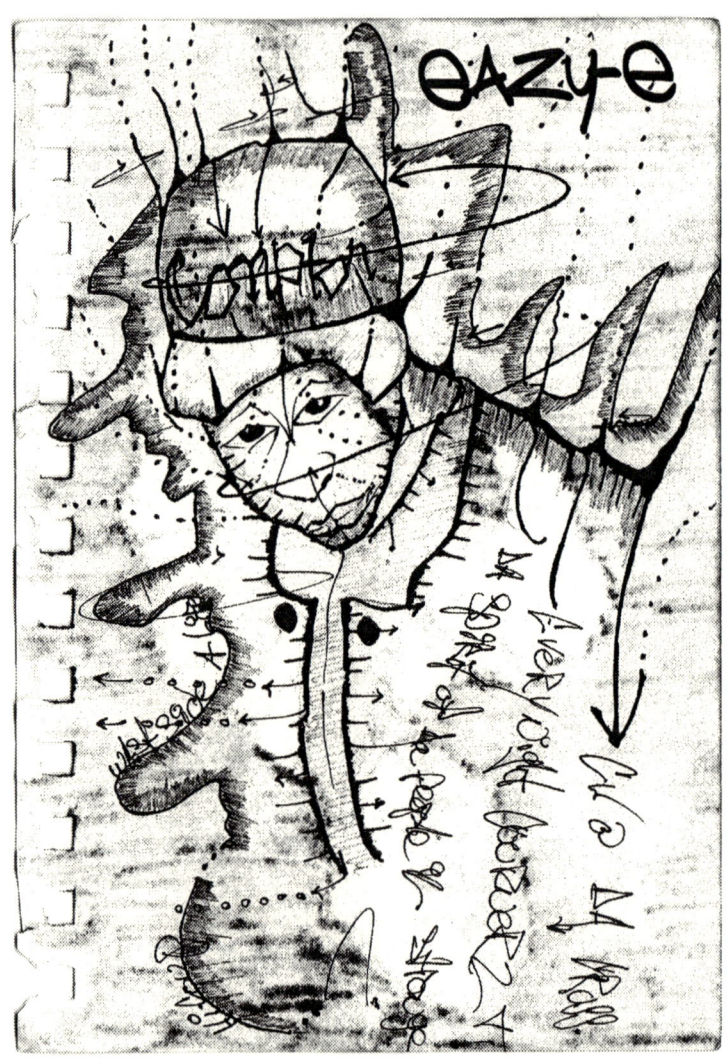

Name: Eazy-E
Government Name: Eric Wright
Label: Founded **Ruthless Records**
Stomping Grounds: Compton, CA
Intelligence: Eazy's impact on music in general is probably underestimated. From the very beginning he wanted to create his own record label. Eazy used money he made on the street selling drugs plus money he inherited from a relative to start **Ruthless Records**. The group cut the single "Boyz-N-Da Hood" and traveled around Compton dropping off records with a card. The record exploded when Greg Mack from the L.A. radio station K-Day suggested they clean up the lyrics. If they did so he promised to give it a shot. Mack had the record within a day. The song went on to become the soundtrack for the streets.

As a result of Eazy's visionary approach **Ruthless** quickly grew to become one of the most successful independent record labels in music history, not just rap history. He is responsible for starting the careers of several artists including Ice Cube, Dr. Dre, Above the Law, the D.O.C. and Bone Thugs-N-Harmony. Eazy also masterminded separate major label distribution deals for his various artists in order to maximize revenue. Among aficionados he's regarded as the godfather of Gangsta Rap.

Name: RZA
Government Name: Robert F. Diggs
Label: Wu-Tang Productions
Stomping Grounds: Staten Island, NY
Intelligence: After being dropped from **Tommy Boy** and going on a year long hiatus, the RZA (formerly Prince Rakeem) formed Wu-Tang Productions and released *Protect Ya Neck/After the Laughter* independently. RZA's nine-man crew then pressed up five hundred copies of the single and sold it directly to record stores and DJs. On the heels of the single's underground success the RZA set forth his now-famous five-year plan. For five years he would creatively and commercially guide the careers of the entire clan. After that the members would be free to choose their own creative direction. Using his botched experiences with **Tommy Boy** (and the GZA's equally abysmal experience on **Cold Chillin'**) as his guide, he signed an unprecedented group deal with **Loud Records** that allowed the individual Wu-Tang members to sign independent deals with other labels. The RZA's plan to house his artists on different labels in order to create a competitive market with Wu-Tang members at the center reaping the financial rewards was risky to say the least. The plan, nevertheless, worked out brilliantly and the Wu-Tang brand became one of the most profitable and recognizable brands in hip-hop history. It has since been parlayed into fashion, comic books, film, and video game merchandising.

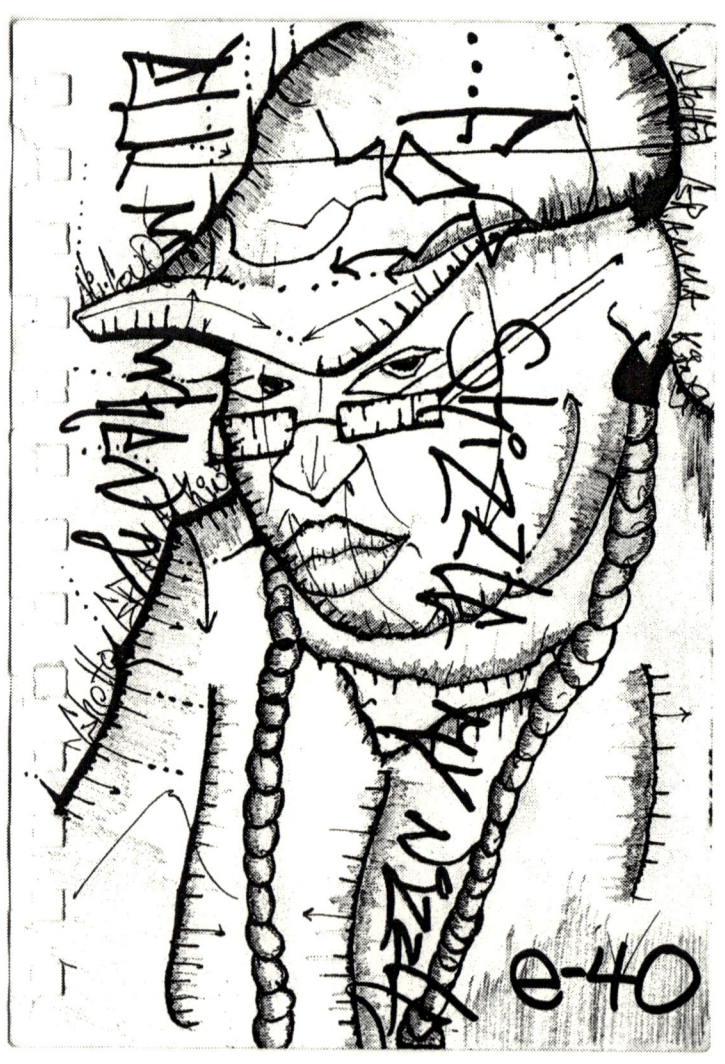

Name: E-40

Government Name: Earl Stevens

Label: Sic Wid It Records

Stomping grounds: Vallejo, CA

Intelligence: Along with his cousin b-legit, founded **Sic Wid it Records** and tapes in the late '80s after dropping out of college. Was inspired by his Uncle Charles and fellow bay area rapper Too $hort to push his music independently. 40 sold all his tapes and records out of the back of his car and did all his own promotion and marketing. 40 and his cousin put their music on consignment at liquor stores, barber shops, tire and rim shops. They drove up and down the coast to swap meets. They sent tapes to their family members in Louisiana and Texas. Pretty soon they were moving hundreds of thousands of tapes without a major distributor. 40's 1994 EP, *The Mailman*, hit #4 on R&B Billboard 200, which was unheard of. 40 and the Click signed with **Jive** in 1994 and released nine albums with the label before signing with **Universal** in 2006.

Name: Master P
Government Name: Percy Robert Miller
Label: No Limit Records
Stomping grounds: Oakland, CA and New Orleans, LA

Intelligence: Following in the footsteps of Too $hort and E-40, Master P sold his LP *The Ghetto's Tryin' to Kill Me!* and the EP *99 Ways to Die* strictly through independent outlets. He traveled around the country to any and all cities and towns where he thought his music would find a market. One of his most savvy guerilla marketing techniques was giving out free samples of his music to guys with the fanciest cars in the neighborhood. He understood that local trendsetters would open the door for him. The albums sold a combined 250,000 copies and paved the way for P to sign a distribution deal with Priority Records that allowed him to keep 85% of the royalties from record sales and all his publishing rights. This was unheard of at the time. From there P built a highly identifiable brand that stood over and above the particular artist being marketed. He cross-promoted his artists to maximize their visibility and expand their respective audiences. And he inflated demand by ensuring his artists would debut at #1 on Soundscan.

Name: Ani Difranco
Government Name: Angela Marie Difranco
Label: Righteous Babe Records
Stomping Grounds: Buffalo, NY
Intelligence: Avowed Socialist/Anarchist, DiFranco was once quoted as saying, "The Way to your future is independent." Though she isn't a rapper (she's a folk singer if you didn't already know), she is a staunchly independent and successful artistpreneur. At eighteen DiFranco started her own record label and put out her first album. For the last decade-and-a-half she has toured and recorded extensively. She has sold hundreds of thousands of records through independent means and relationships she's developed with independent distributors around the world. She writes, publishes, records, releases and creates the artwork for her albums. To date she has recorded 18 studio albums, 12 live albums, and 3 EPs.

AFTERWORD
BY JEREMY GLICK

Afterword: Just a little room so my family can breathe [in Hell]

"Until Amiri Baraka came along, Jazz was entirely written about by white people, they were the 'experts' of the music. That writing about Jazz, professing expert knowledge of the other—it works as a form of control. It freezes Jazz out of the urban context it came out of, we have to check for this tendency in hip-hop".
-Jazz pianist Vijay Iyer

It is imperative that practitioners, partisans, and all-day-every-day lovers of Hip- Hop step their game up in terms of contributing to the creation of a multi-faceted literature on the music. Testimonial from people in the game, an account of the business end— practical application/How To as well as analytic (the political economy of hip-hop music), political analysis around form/content, and aesthetics of the form (as Amiri Baraka wrote about the beboppers in the jazz era—in the last instance what Matters most is HOW YOU SOUND!!!). Without a concise accounting of all aspects of the music, we run smack up against the danger of letting a discourse be crafted as cooptation, corporate market viability, and meaningless fluff by people who don't have the best interest of the music and the communities in which they originated at hand (or at least in their hearts and ever expanding off-shore bank accounts). Culture workers need to redefine and reformulate the language used to frame discussion around hip-hop—like Creature and Dax-Devlon Ross do for the notion of the hustle, or for that matter how the RBG/People's Army Camp effectively have transformed pimpin' from signifying the brutal exploitation of women by men to a commentary on how we all get our surplus labor extracted and exploited [some more than others for concrete historical not mystical reasons] in monopoly capitalism. It's key for the artists and fans to do it themselves and generate a literature comparable to the legacy left by Jazz generations—captured in such books as Mingus's *Beneath the Underdog*, Ellington's *Music is My Muse*, A.B. Spellman's *5 Lives in BeBop* and Baraka's entire work. Jeff Chang's *Can't Stop Won't Stop* history of hip-hop and Stic Man's *The Art of Emceeing* are both welcome correctives filling up this gap. Creature and Dax-Devlon Ross push along this forward moving trend.

We can't just rely on the magazine industry, as much as they help lubricate our pockets [including mine, every now and then]. Quite frankly—Magazine articles are often too wed to questions of commerce to be a reliable archive of any culture [let alone hip-hop]. Either they have a financial stake in advertising from record companies or journalists trade ink for cultural capital and admittance to certain coveted, cool-kid scenes. Anti-establishment zines with revolutionary political agendas often court the same coterie of artists familiar to activist movements so usual suspects get all the shine. All of a sudden revolutionary orgs are looking towards musicians to craft a transformative agenda instead of the other way around. Either way you slice it--

Working class artists, as Creature would say "Regular" folk stories get Chubb Rocked—i.e. lost in the storm.

Revolutionary practice, revolutionary art, a revolutionary ethic in the last instance only has two end games—the accumulation of the resources you need to live a healthy, happy, and full life and self-determination [the ability for communities to control their own destiny—a goal especially key for oppressed nationalities].

In the last instance it is about the dollar. Until that abstract equivalent, magic maker of some and breaker of others gets the ax, we got to hustle collectively to provide for the ability to reproduce our lives—to live better lives. Abundance for our friends and our family is the goal--abundance which does not come off the back, sweat, and blood of most of the working people on the planet. And no rant against marketing or commerce from some middle class anarchist yelled from atop a very heated, very plush dorm room at NYU is going to make much difference no matter. On that note, neither will some well intended but misguided rant about the Illuminati or reptilians in people clothing (which lacks the precision and class analysis of Malcolm's more thoughtful discussion of wolves and sheep).

Creature's grind, Creature's hustle, Creature's humility is the constant reminder that the struggle to live a better life where we live is all bound up in the constant pursuit to get that dollar--To get it, until we can mature collectively enough to get beyond it. Never forgetting like the German poet Bertolt Brecht thinking about a different time and place, the responsibility to describe with precision where we live, why we hustle, to have enough courage to call it by its real name:

On thinking about Hell, I gather
My brother Shelley found it was a place
Much like the city of London. I
Who live in Los Angeles and not in London
Find, on thinking about Hell, that it must be
Still more like Los Angeles.

The common bind between these two cities and epochs-

The Houses in Hell, too, are not all ugly.
But the fear of being thrown on the streets
Wears down the inhabitants of the villas no less than
The inhabitants of the shanty towns.[2]

---

[2] "On Thinking about Hell" Brecht, Bertolt. Poems 1913-1956 (NY: Methuen), 1976, p. 367.

CREATURE'S ACKNOWLEDGEMENTS

Blessings to Allah, Mom and Dad, my sisters and brothers, my nephew Aziz (you are the future), all my cousins and Aunts and Uncles, and any other family members I might've missed.

Special thanks to all the people who contributed to this book. Dax, without you I would not have been able to do this. You are a very talented brother. Thank you. Jeremy Glick, Percee P (your wisdom is necessary), Duo Live, Logan P. McCoy, Shake-O Blaize, Preachermann, Marvo, Unknown, Sensational, Subcon, H. the Great and all of the independent Artispreneurs. Thanks especially to Commander in Chicago for hippin' me to that term.

Thanks to Mike Ladd, Rob Sonic, Fredones, Tme, Slug, Busdriver, Beans, L-evitate, Alyssa, Skila, Sinnagi, Gab Gacha, and Scaborogh.

Thanks to All of the people I have had countless talking marathons with about music, life, love and everything in between.

To Corona Queens, (AKA Crown City) for the years of inspiration.

To New York City for being homebase

To Calle Cardona hold ya head!

I know I've missed some people and some places. Blame it on the mind and not the heart.

Be Safe and Stay Up,

Creature--

DAX'S ACKNOWLEDGEMENTS

Creature, you believed when you didn't have to. Thank you.

Percee P., Logan P. McCoy, Hi-Coup, Duo Live, Derek Beres. Your fingerprints are all over this book. It would not be what it is without your time, your support and your voices and visions. Thank you.

One,
DX

CREATURE'S DISCOGRAPHY

2007 Creature– *Hustle To Be Free*– Coffee Grind Media

2006 Baba & Yako– Split Consciousness– *Beat Box/Dub Poetic*– Open Thought Productions

2006 CoreRhythm– Ebony Eyes– *Nat Turner Reloaded*– Spixmatic

2006 Chong Nee– Suicidal– *Just Getting By on Love*– Handmade Records

2005 Creature. *Never Say Die*– Coffee Grind Media

2005 Rob Sonic– Sniper Picnic– *Tony Hawk's American Wasteland*– Def Jux

2004 MF Doom–Open Mic Nite 2– *Viktor Vaughn Vaudeville Villain*– Sound Ink Records

2003 FredOnes– The Same Still– *Phobia of Doors*– Raptivism

2002 Dr. Israel– Boots, Culture, Murder– *Black Rose Liberation*– Baboon

2001 Sound Ink– Human Error– *Colapsus*– Sound Ink Records

2000 Creature– *Deja Taboo*– Insomniac Dream

2000 Gunn Hill Road– The Precious Theme– *Infesticons*– Big Dada

1997 X- ectutioners– The Cipher– *X-Pressions*– Aspodel

1996 Triflicts– *Genuine/Don't Make Me Try*– Hydra Records

Printed in the United States
200257BV00007B/76/A